A MOMENT
for PRAYER

Got a moment? That's all it takes to reach out to God in prayer!

A Moment for Prayer is the perfect book to keep at your bedside, on your kitchen table, at your workplace, or next to your favorite chair. Pick it up, turn to any of the 365 simple prayers, and reach out to God.

The prayers and short verses from scripture are complete in themselves. Each one lifts a thought, care, or concern to God. It may be all you need to say, or it may be the beginning of a much longer, deeper conversation. Either way, may these words strengthen you and assure you of God's continuing love for you throughout all the moments of your day.

In the morning, in the evening, or anytime in between, bless yourself with a moment for prayer!

D0039761

A Moment for Prayer
ISBN 978-0-9828555-3-9

Published by Product Concept Mfg., Inc.
2175 N. Academy Circle #200, Colorado Springs, CO 80909

©2011 Product Concept Mfg., Inc. All rights reserved.

Written and Compiled by Patricia Mitchell
in association with Product Concept Mfg., Inc.

All scripture quotations are from the King James version
of the Bible unless otherwise noted.

Scriptures taken from the Holy Bible,
New International Version®, NIV®.
Copyright © 1973, 1978, 1984, 2010 by Biblica, Inc.™
Used by permission of Zondervan.
All rights reserved worldwide.
www.zondervan.com

1

Today my calendar is full, and I'm feeling overwhelmed with things I need to do! Dear God, teach me how to possess the **SERENITY** I yearn for... the peace of mind and heart I so desire. Even in the middle of my hectic day, lead me to that place of inner refreshment where I can rest at ease in You.

He restoreth my soul.
Psalm 23:3

2

[decorative illustration]

God, so much is going on in my life that it's often hard for me to sort out what is important and what is unimportant. Please grant me the **INSIGHT** I need to identify those things that are worthwhile and meaningful... those things that truly deserve my time and attention. Clear my vision so I may focus on these things.

Get wisdom: and with all thy getting get understanding.
Proverbs 4:7

3

Sometimes I'm at a loss to know what to do next. God, please provide me with Your **GUIDANCE** as I make decisions, set priorities, and go about the activities of my day. Even when things do not turn out my way, keep my heart confident that Your path is the best one for me to follow.

Thy word is a lamp unto my feet,
and a light unto my path.
Psalm 119:105

4

So many things promise temporary happiness, but only You provide true, long-lasting **JOY**. Dear God, show me the difference! Open my heart so I may possess the deep, fulfilling joy that comes with the peace of Your presence and the assurance of Your love. Help me find the joy that will stay with me forever.

Rejoice in the Lord.
Philippians 4:4

5

God, enable me to be a **BLESSING** to others today. In my smile, let them see the warmth of a loving heart; and in my words, the caring of a thoughtful friend. Through my actions, may those around me receive the help, understanding, and encouragement they need. Where I am, let the gift of Your love and compassion reach out to all.

Where I am, there shall also my servant be.
John 12:26

6

Dear God, grant me **COURAGE** as I meet life's trials and troubles. Keep me from attempting to avoid my responsibilities, even if they prove difficult to bear; or from trying to run away from challenges that are mine to overcome. Instead, let these things enable me to grow in strength and in faith, confidence, and trust in You.

Be strong and of a good courage.
Deuteronomy 31:6

7

It seems I'm always asking You for something, God, but seldom remembering to thank You for all the gifts You have given to me. So today I want to say a special prayer of **THANKS** for the blessings I possess... for the special blessings that make my heart leap for joy, and for the everyday blessings that bring me comfort and pleasure. Thank You!

In every thing give thanks.
1 Thessalonians 5:18

8

In all I say and do, let my **MOTIVATION** be pleasing to You, dear God. Keep me from seeking anything other than what will work to the benefit of others and build in me spiritual strength and confidence pleasing to You. Purify my heart and enable me to act in sincerity and truth.

Serve him in sincerity and in truth.
Joshua 24:14

9 God, bless my **LOVED ONES** and all those close to me in friendship. Cover them with Your protection, guide them in their endeavors, grant them their deepest desires, and provide them with everything they need for their well-being and happiness. Surround them now and always with Your presence and Your love.

The LORD bless thee, and keep thee.
Numbers 6:24

10 Dear God, help me overcome the habit of complaining about things beyond my control. Teach me instead the way of **ACCEPTANCE**, and grant me understanding so I may focus my thoughts and place my efforts where I can help and heal... where I have the ability to offer solutions, assistance, and encouragement.

Do all things without murmurings and disputing.
Philippians 2:14

11

Today I pray for spiritual and physical **HEALTH**. As I choose good things for my body, grant me the wisdom to choose good things for my mental and emotion health, too. Keep me from habits, desires, or addictions that would harm me, and open to me the help or counsel I need to live each day in the best possible way.

Your body is the temple of the Holy Spirit, who is in you.
1 Corinthians 6:19 NIV

12

Dear God, teach me to **WAIT** with patience! When things aren't going as quickly as I think they should, I worry and fret instead of simply holding on and waiting for Your purpose to reveal itself. Remind me that all things will happen according to Your timetable, not mine; and according to Your purpose.

Blessed are all they that wait for him.
Isaiah 30:18

13

In the hustle and bustle of my day...when I'm thinking of a thousand things at once...remind me, God, to "stop and smell the roses." Open my eyes to the priceless value of **THIS MOMENT**, and show me the wonders that surround me every day. Let me utter a heartfelt "thank You" for the miracles present in each moment of life.

The earth is full of the goodness of the LORD.
Psalm 33:5

14

Though some people seem to take pleasure in predicting the worst possible outcome of any situation, I want to choose differently. God, I look to You for help in finding the **SILVER LINING** in the events taking place. Make me willing to uplift and encourage others with Your words of truth and hope.

A word fitly spoken is like apples of gold in pictures of silver.
Proverbs 25:11

15

It's tempting for me to imagine that my **THOUGHTS** are private and known only to myself. Yet, God, You see everything, even the deepest stirrings of my heart. Pour Your light within me, and help me banish unhealthy and unproductive thoughts from my mind. Let my heart be the home of right thinking, good judgment, and positive attitudes.

Create in me a clean heart, O God.
Psalm 51:10

16

Thank You for the presence in my life of those who can laugh at life's situations! Could I be like them, God? Grant me, I pray, the gift of **HUMOR**... the kind of humor that builds people up... relaxes the heart...brings out the smiles... and smoothes rough paths. From the example of others, teach me how to cultivate a light and merry heart.

He that is of a merry heart hath a continual feast.
Proverbs 15:15

17

The fast pace of our age and all its attractions leave little time for spiritual things. But God, I want to change that. I want to develop a deep and vibrant **INNER LIFE**... a life touched by the hand of Your inspiration, enlivened by imagination and creativity, and marked by faith in You. Help me make time in my day for You.

Do not conform to the pattern of this world,
but be transformed by the renewing of your mind.
Romans 12:2 NIV

18 When confrontation arises between me and another person, I'm not sure how to handle myself. God, I pray for **UNDERSTANDING** so I may know how to answer those whose words may hurt me and how to work toward peace when conflict crosses my path. Especially in challenging situations, enable me to be aware of and respond to others' points of view.

Seek peace, and pursue it.
Psalm 34:14

19 God, sometimes it's hard to keep going. When the task is difficult, or the project is not progressing well, I become discouraged and I want to quit. Yet I know I am failing others and failing myself! That's why I'm asking for the blessing of **PERSEVERANCE.** Help me keep going to the end so I may enjoy the reward and fulfillment of finishing the work that is mine.

O God, strengthen my hands.
Nehemiah 6:9

20 It's the "information age," and I get so much information that I don't know what to make of it! I'm praying today, God, for the gift of **CLARITY** in my thinking so I can sort out truth from falsehood... fact from fluff. Keep me from being swayed by those who would deceive me; but enable me to encourage, help, and support those who speak the truth.

Buy the truth, and sell it not.
Proverbs 23:23

21 When I see someone in need, God, let me be the one to **REACH OUT** and help. Grant me the ability and willingness to listen when others share their sorrows... to give practical assistance where needed... to be the one others can depend on to be there, no matter what. In all ways, let my heart be the one that cares.

Bear ye one another's burdens.
Galatians 6:2

22

When I'm faced with difficult or significant life **DECISIONS**, God, it's hard to know what to do. Shall I choose this path or that path? Shall I turn this way or that? I pray for Your help! Help me think things through, make my choices according to Your guidance, and then walk ahead with courage and confidence.

Choose you this day whom ye will serve.
Joshua 24:15

23

It's so easy to do just enough to get by...to work no harder than necessary... to put in no more effort than it takes to get the job out. But You, God, have put in my heart a **HIGHER VISION**. Strengthen me and enliven me that I may strive to do my best and give my best in whatever task I undertake. In this, may I find the satisfaction of a job well done.

He which soweth sparingly shall reap also sparingly.
2 Corinthians 9:6

24

As I seek to know more about You, God, I meet people with many different perceptions of You. Guide me as I listen to them and think about what they are saying; then be with me as I determine my own **BELIEFS**. May my values and principles echo Your voice and correspond to Your message.

Believe not every spirit, but try the spirits whether they are of God.
1 John 4:1

25 God, help me take time to **LISTEN!** When my loved ones are speaking, I may find myself thinking of a dozen other things. When my friends share their cares with me, I realize that at times I'm hardly hearing what they are saying. Please enable me to give my undivided attention to those who are talking to me. Teach me, God, how to really listen.

Speak, LORD; for thy servant heareth.
1 Samuel 3:9

26 There's something that seems to get lost once the growing up years are gone, and that's the spirit of **DISCOVERY**. Children take such delight in finding and learning about new things! God, banish my grown-up fears and grant me a child-like spirit of discovery... a heart of wonder and acceptance... an eye for all the tiny, whimsical, enchanting things You have created in the world.

The heavens declare the glory of God;
the skies proclaim the work of his hands.
Psalm 19:1 NIV

27 God, help me remain true to my **PRINCIPLES**. Sure, it's easy to *imagine* I'd stand up for my values come what may; but I know the power of the *real* world. Please give me the inner strength and the conviction to put principle over popularity... high standards over easy gain...Your guidance over others' opinions. Help me, God, be true to myself.

What good is it for someone to gain the whole world, yet forfeit their soul?
Mark 8:36 NIV

28 Insecurity is hard to fight against. In certain situations, I find myself trying to compensate for my shortcomings by acting like a know-it-all, but inside I know I'm faking. Help me, God, have the guts to admit when I don't know, and grant me the **HONESTY** to ask for assistance when I need it. This is the way of true confidence.

Be careful to do what is right in the eyes of everyone.
Romans 12:17 NIV

29

Dear God, help me distance myself from illusions and imaginings about my life, my convictions, my relationships, my place in the world. Grant me the **SELF-KNOWLEDGE** it takes to face reality and see myself as others see me. Where there is weakness, grant me strength; and where there is goodness, let me humbly give thanks to You.

Deceive not yourselves.
Jeremiah 37:9

30

I'm tempted to want for myself what others have and what I see around me. Yet I know all these things are not essential and not everything will enhance or enrich my life. When I'm faced with desire, turn my heart toward **CONTENTMENT** with those things You have provided for my benefit and for the benefit of my loved ones. Turn my desire, God, to You.

Be content with such things as ye have.
Hebrews 13:5

31

Though I live in a culture that exalts material things, teach me to desire spiritual treasures. Inspire me to yearn for the riches of the heart rather than the trappings of the world, and to show by my daily **PRIORITIES** and choices that You come first in my life. Let me de-clutter my life to make room for You.

Seek ye first the kingdom of God,
and his righteousness.
Matthew 6:33

32

Dear God, I have so many **HOPES AND DREAMS** for my future! But in all of these, I desire to seek Your guidance and to stay on the path You have laid before me. May the things I would like to have happen in my life always take second place to what You send. Shape my hopes and dreams, and let them reflect Your good and gracious will.

In all thy ways acknowledge him, and he shall
direct thy paths.
Proverbs 3:6

33

Thank You, God, for those close to me. Teach me to cherish my **RELATIONSHIPS**, because the caring people You put into my life allow me to give and receive... to love and be loved...to help and be helped in return. Bless the ties that keep us together in family and friendship; and may we always be a blessing to one another.

We are members one of another.
Ephesians 4:25

34

Dear God, open the eyes of my heart to see and appreciate the **LITTLE BLESSINGS** that are around me every day. Let me delight in the sunshine and stand in awe of the starry skies. Enable me to take equal delight in the clouds that float across the heavens and the snowflake that falls toward the earth. In all these things, I thank and praise You!

Rejoice in every good thing which the LORD thy god hath given unto thee.
Deuteronomy 26:11

35

It has been said that we get what we expect. If this is true, God, then fill my heart and mind with **EXPECTATIONS** in keeping with what You desire for me. Keep me away from negative thinking, and instead guide me toward an outlook based on what's real, along with a trusting reliance on Your continuing control over all that happens.

Thy lovingkindness is better than life.
Psalm 63:3

36

OPTIMISTS look on the bright side of things, and this is the kind of person I would like to be. God, I want to be the one who looks at what's wrong and works to fix it... the one who looks at what could be better and sees the possibilities for making it wonderful. That's what people with an optimistic attitude do—God, grant me the blessing of being among them!

We are troubled on every side, yet not distressed; we are perplexed, but not in despair.
2 Corinthians 4:8

37

I need Your **COMFORT**, God, because only Your comfort reaches where it hurts. In times of anxiety, pain, or loss, Your comfort soothes my heart of its wounds and gives solace to my spiritual loneliness. Nothing the world can offer can give me the kind of comfort I need for true, deep, long-lasting healing.

I will not leave you comfortless: I will come to you.
John 14:18

38

In places where wars and battles rage, I pray for **PEACE.** May those who destroy become like those who build up; may those who lash out in anger turn to the ways of those who seek compromise for the good of all. In every way I can, God, enable me to work toward a world where peace reigns among all people.

Blessed are the peacemakers: for they shall be called the children of God.
Matthew 5:9

39

Thank You, God, for the assurance of Your presence and Your love in my life. When I'm feeling down, remembering that You care for me is just the kind of **AFFIRMATION** I need to lift me up again and help me go on with my day. "You are with me today" is all I need to say to remind myself of Your ever-present love!

God is love.
1 John 4:16

40

How misguided to imagine that spiritual people should look serious all the time! On the contrary, You have given those who love You the freedom to laugh, love, sing, dance, play, pray, create...all **PLEASURES** reserved for the light heart, the kindly soul, the child-like spirit. Thank You, God, for all the joyful pleasures of life!

Whoso trusteth in the LORD, happy is he.
Proverbs 16:20

41

Despite all the knowledge here on Earth, Your knowledge surpasses it all. For this reason, God, I come to You when I'm looking for **ANSWERS** to the questions that distress or perplex me. Help me understand the response You give in whatever way you choose to send it... and most of all, help me accept it in faith and trust.

The will of the Lord be done.
Acts 21:14

42

Dear God, it's so easy to rely on money, success, or personal achievement for security. It's easy to think these things will bring real protection, but they will not, and never have. Only You, God, are the source of safety for my spirit and the sure provider for my life. Help me **LEAN ON YOU** for my sure and steady foundation.

It is better to trust in the LORD than to put confidence in man.
Psalm 118:8

43

Sometimes I lose the ability to see beyond my **PROBLEMS**. They take over my thoughts and my time to the point that I dwell on them night and day! God, remove this habit from me, and grant me a right perspective on the challenges facing me. Expand my vision, lighten my heart, and guide me toward meaningful and lasting solutions.

The LORD is good, a strong hold in the day of trouble.
Nahum 1:7

44

TODAY, dear God, let my heart and mind focus on You. I need not make great claims for the future, and You do not ask for promises I cannot keep. This moment, this day, are what counts... and it is now that I dedicate to You in prayer, praise, and gratitude for all the blessings this day will bring.   .

Let us be glad and rejoice, and give honour to him.
Revelation 19:7

45

As my body needs **REST**, so does my spirit. Yet when I can't get away to a place of calm and repose, You come to me with Your gentle presence. You enter my heart in a moment, and You fill it with tranquility. You speak to my spirit in soothing words, and I am quieted. In You, God, my rest is complete.

You will find rest for your souls.
Matthew 11:29 NIV

46

God, please grant me the blessing of **HAPPY MEMORIES**. Let the good times with friends and family, the joys and celebrations among loved ones, and the companionship and encouragement I have received from so many people fill my mind and heart. In fond remembrances, let me find my treasure.

Forget not the LORD thy God.
Deuteronomy 8:11

47

I've been taught to say "thank you" when someone does something nice, but how often I forget! For the thoughtful word, the encouraging smile, the pat on the back, I find myself forgetting to go back to that person and show my **APPRECIATION**. I ask You, God, to keep me mindful of the caring people in my life. Bless them, I pray, today and always.

Withhold not good from them to whom it is due.
Proverbs 3:27

48

"Let go and let God" the saying reads, but I find it difficult to do. **LETTING GO** takes trust, and for an increased measure of trust I pray to You. Enable me to rely on You with such certainty that I will hand over to You my deepest worries, my dearest dreams, my fondest hopes. Help me let go and let God!

We trust in the living God.
1 Timothy 4:10

49

When working with others on a complex project, **DIFFICULTIES** crop up. Perhaps there's a clash of personalities, or an unforeseen hitch in the process. At these times, God, enable me to step back and ask for Your help. I pray for an even temper, helpful suggestions, and most of all, words that empower everyone to work toward our common goal.

Call upon me in the day of trouble:
I will deliver thee.
Psalm 50:15

50

God, You have created me with certain skills, talents, interests, and abilities. Thank You for these blessings, and I pray for the desire to use them to their fullest for my benefit and for the well-being of others. Keep self-pride far from me, and keep me from comparing myself with others. Let my **INDIVIDUALITY** shine through in the gifts you have given me.

There are diversities of gifts, but the same Spirit.
1 Corinthians 12:4

51

With each year that passes, I gain more and more **EXPERIENCE** with myself, with others, and with the world. As others have supported me in the past, God, I want to use the experience I have gained so far to assist those who are coming up after me. Put in my path, I pray, people who could benefit from my help and counsel.

Grow in grace, and in the knowledge of our Lord.
2 Peter 3:18

52

It has been said that our true **CHARACTER** is revealed in how we act when no one's looking. Dear God, this is where I would like to grow. Even when I think I'm unseen, enable me to do the right thing. Even when I imagine it doesn't matter, teach me to say the right words. And even in small matters, please help me give my best effort. Grant me the blessing of a strong and good character.

There is nothing covered, that shall not be revealed; and hid, that shall not be known.
Matthew 10:26

53

As a good tree bears good fruit, dear God, help me produce **"GOOD FRUIT"** in the things I say and do, and in the way I live. Fill my thoughts with Your Spirit so my actions will prove consistent, useful, and practical. Let the "good fruit" I bear come from a heart and mind firmly rooted in Your message of love for all people.

Every good tree bringeth forth good fruit.
Matthew 7:17

54

The purpose of an **ADVENTURE** is to see and do new things. Crossing the boundaries of routine energizes mind and body, offering fresh insights and exciting discoveries about ourselves and the world. Dear God, open my heart to the adventure of getting to know You better and of following Your will and plans for my life. It is the adventure of a lifetime!

Come ye after me.
Mark 1:17

55

You are all about **LOVE**... love for me, love for others, love for the world. With love, God, let the eyes of my spirit look out each day. Allow me to perceive You in me and in the faces of everyone I meet; enable me to discover love, even in unpromising places...for it is there. Love is everywhere, because You are.

God so loved the world.
John 3:16

56

Who said, "Words can never hurt me"? Certainly not You, God! You know the power of **WORDS**... their power to wound the heart and crush the spirit. For this reason You tell us to speak carefully and kindly, and to choose our words well. I pray for this ability, God...the ability to speak good words.

Let your gentleness be evident to all.
Philippians 4:5 NIV

57

No matter how old I am, God, or how much I think I know, I pray this: Keep me **TEACHABLE**. Never let me imagine I have no need to learn from others... from children as well as adults, from the simplest as well as the wisest. God, grant me the willingness to remain a learner all my life...most especially a learner eager to learn from You.

A wise man will hear, and will increase learning...
Proverbs 1:5

58

Dear God, you put **OPPORTUNITIES** in front of me every day. Please help me be aware of them! When I think nothing is working out, focus my eyes on the openings available to me, especially the unexpected and hidden opportunities that I miss. Guide me, please, as I continue on my path!

Knock, and it shall be opened unto you.
Luke 11:9

59 There's **EXCELLENCE** in following your ways, God, when those who love You seek to do Your will. I strive for this kind of excellence. Through Your presence in my life, may my words and actions be helpful to others and pleasing to You. In the deepest corners of my heart, God, will excellence prevail, because in the deepest corners of my heart, You will dwell.

The LORD loveth the righteous.
Psalm 146:8

60 Without "thinking outside the box" sometimes, life becomes bounded in old habits and stale routines. I know, God, this is not what You have in mind for me! Grant me a willingness to discover and explore new ways of doing things. Strengthen the wings of my spirit and let me soar to fresh horizons. Open the delights of **CREATIVITY** to me.

The desire accomplished is sweet to the soul.
Proverbs 13:19

61

Dear God, there are things that keep me up at night... things I toss around in my mind... things I worry about. Deliver me from these feelings of **ANXIETY**. Help me depend on You instead of thinking everything depends on me. Take my worries and replace them with Your words of assurance and Your promise of strength and protection. In You I put my trust!

Let not your heart be troubled,
neither let it be afraid.
John 14:27

62

It's only two words—**I'M SORRY**—yet sometimes they're the hardest words to say. Help me speak these words when I have offended anyone by being abrupt or short-tempered; or when I have treated anyone unkindly. And help me also speak these words to You, God, with a humble heart... a heart ready to return to You in truth.

As ye would that men should do to you,
do ye also to them likewise.
Luke 6:31

63

I desire, God, to speak and act with **RESPECT** for others. Even when I hear opinions I don't agree with, I want to set an example of civility and reason. Help me to reign in my emotions and find common ground between myself and others. In my attitude, let them know they are worthy, as am I, of recognition, respect, and dignity.

Let us therefore make every effort to do what leads to peace...
Romans 14:19 NIV

64

What do You see, God? You see the universe... the world... the past... the present. Yes, You see all of this, and more! Your great view reminds me that my **VISION** is limited and small. When I start to tell You exactly what I want for my future, remind me that You are in a far better position to know my tomorrow than anyone. You, God, are the one who sees all.

We fix our eyes not on what is seen, but on what is unseen. For what is seen is temporary, but what is unseen is eternal.
2 Corinthians 4:18 NIV

65 Sometimes I need to review the basics! When I speak rudely on the phone simply because I can't see the person, remind me, God, that the voice on the other end of the line is a human being, just like me. No matter how many electronic gadgets and conveniences come into my home, let me never forget the need for **POLITENESS** in speech. Let me remember the importance of basic courtesy and graciousness.

Let your speech be always with grace, seasoned with salt.
Colossians 4:6

66 Do my **ACTIONS** match my intentions? I ask You, God, to look down and see. Open my eyes to areas where I am failing to close the gap between what I do and what I want to do... to times when I fall back on who I used to be, instead of who I am today in You. Please grant me the ability to follow more closely Your directions and Your will.

Since we live by the Spirit, let us keep in step with the Spirit.
Galatians 5:25 NIV

67

How I long for peace of mind, the **STILLNESS** of spirit that would let me sleep! God, deliver me from the clutches of anxiety and fear, so I may rest in confidence that You will keep me safe. I know in all things You will work for my benefit, and I know You will never fail me. Please bring me peaceful dreams and restful sleep.

Be still, and know that I am God.
Psalm 46:10

68

Dear God, I ask You, the source of all wisdom, for **ENLIGHTENMENT**. Clear my mind of all distracting thoughts that pull me down and confuse my purpose. According to Your will, grant me the ability to understand spiritual things and to perceive earthly things from a spiritual point of view. Allow me, I pray, to see as You see.

He that followeth me shall not walk in darkness, but shall have the light of life.
John 8:12

69

When I'm in the middle of a dilemma, God, I have a hard time finding my way out. Yet I know You have made a path for me... a **BRIDGE** from darkness to light, from worry to freedom. Please open my eyes so I may see the way in front of me and walk it with assurance, knowing You are there beside me.

Teach me thy way, O LORD, and lead me in a plain path.
Psalm 27:11

70

Someone I love has hurt me deeply, God, and I have a hard time forgiving. Sure, I said the words with my mouth, but my heart was not moved. To this day, I harbor the hurt of that hour. Fill my heart with understanding and acceptance, God, and enable me to **FORGIVE** from the depths of my being, for only by forgiving others can I receive forgiveness from You.

If ye forgive not men their trespasses, neither will your Father forgive your trespasses.
Matthew 6:15

71

You look with mercy on all You have created, God. Please provide me with a measure of Your **COMPASSION** for all living beings. Move me to pray for their needs and to help with practical assistance and useful advice. Let my compassions, stemming from Yours, ease the tension and sufferings present in my corner of the world.

Shew mercy and compassions every man to his brother.
Zechariah 7:9

72

Thank You for the blessing of meaningful **WORK**. In all I do, help me realize the satisfaction of work that is in accordance with Your plan for my life. Where work proves unsatisfying, I pray for new opportunities and challenges; where there is no work, I pray for open doors in the area of my expertise. I pray for all those who work to find fulfillment in their jobs, and for those who are seeking work, God, please guide their paths to the right opportunities.

And whatsoever ye do, do it heartily, as to the Lord, and not unto men.
Colossians 3:23

73

You know the powers and the limitations of my body, God, for You have created it! Help me attain the right level of physical **FITNESS** to keep me as healthy as I can be. Give me the commitment and perseverance I need to eat nutritious foods and exercise, and bless me with Your continued protection of both body and soul.

Before I formed thee in the belly I knew thee.
Jeremiah 1:5

74

Dear God, You have given me the ability and the resources to do many things, but so often I lack the **WILLINGNESS** to act. Please turn my apathy into action and my desire for comfort to a yearning to get involved and make a difference. Grant me the motivation it takes to be a willing presence in the lives of those who need a helping hand.

Let us not become weary in doing good.
Matthew 25:40 NIV

75

So much is accomplished by teamwork, yet so few are productive and enthusiastic team members! God, enable me to foster a spirit of **COOPERATION** among people when I am working in a group. Teach me how to build understanding, encourage collaboration, and assure that all receive their deserved recognition. In this way, God, I desire to be a blessing to others.

Make every effort to keep the unity of the Spirit through the bond of peace.
Ephesians 4:3 NIV

76

You have showered me with blessings, dear God, and now I desire to "pass on" Your great love by practicing **GENEROSITY** to others. Please empower me to shun selfishness, thinking more of another's needs than of my own wants. Let me give without counting the cost... because this is the example You have set for me.

Inasmuch as ye have done it unto one of the least of these my brethren, ye have done it unto me.
Matthew 25:40

77

Change is hard, God, especially when it's unwelcome and unavoidable. What I used to know is passing, and now I'm faced with challenges I never sought out. What can I do? Only this, dear God: lean on You and seek Your strength. Only with Your help can I **EMBRACE NEW**... only with Your vision in front of me will I be able to see goodness come out of unwanted change.

Old things are passed away; behold, all things are become new.
2 Corinthians 5:17

78

As I take a shower in the morning, as I splash my face in the evening, I'm reminded of the **CLEANSING** power of water. In the same way, God, Your cleansing presence refreshes my spirit with forgiveness and grace. The shower of Your merciful goodness washes away all that would harm my relationship with You. May water remind me always of Your work in my life!

The water that I shall give him shall be in him a well of water springing up into everlasting life.
John 4:14

79

Dear God, turn my eyes up to You as I search for **SECURITY** in my beliefs and values. All around me I see the ebb and flow of life, and even my own feelings and ideas change with the times. Why would I look anywhere else but to You—the unchangeable—for true security? Lead me to the shelter of Your presence and Your peace.

In the shadow of thy wings will I make my refuge.
Psalm 57:1

80

Right where I am, dear God, show me Your grace. Open my eyes to the **BEAUTY** of the moment, and make me aware of the goodness all around me. Yes, I get in such a rush sometimes that my days pass like the blur of scenery from the window of a speeding train! God, today... help me see beauty.

Let the beauty of the LORD our God be upon us.
Psalm 90:17

81

How often, dear God, I get caught up trying to impress others! I want to be the first... I want to own the latest and the greatest... I want to be the boss. But I know these things don't impress You at all. What impresses You is a humble heart... a heart that puts others first, is not envious, and knows the **POWER** of contentment. This, God, is truly impressive!

Every way of a man is right in his own eyes: but the LORD pondereth the hearts.
Proverbs 21:2

82

It's easy to sit back and criticize, but less easy to stand up and get involved. Grant me the willingness to **ENGAGE** when something is important to me. Let me put my thoughts and prayers into action, because without action, nothing will change. In big ways and in small ways, God, I want to make a difference.

Let your light so shine before men, that they may see your good works, and glorify your Father which is in heaven.
Matthew 5:16

83

If there is a positive aspect of danger, it's this: because of the dangers all around me, I am moved to search for true **PROTECTION**. I find it with You, God, because You have promised to be my sure and constant defense. Even when I'm in harm's path, You alone have the power to show me the way out. You alone are the source of safety.

He shall give his angels charge over thee,
to keep thee in all thy ways.
Psalm 91:11

84

"If only..." When these words cross my mind, dear God, bring me back to **REALITY**. Grant me, God, the willingness to live for today, confronting its challenges and recognizing its opportunities. Let my prayers come to You from a heart and mind clear of delusion and wishful thinking, for only in reality will I find Your plan for my life.

Take therefore no thought for the morrow:
for the morrow shall take thought for the
things of itself.
Matthew 6:34

85

Excuses, excuses! You don't want to hear them, God, I know. That is why I want to move away from offering excuses to taking **RESPONSIBILITY** for my words and actions. Even when I've stumbled, made an embarrassing mistake, or started down an ill-advised path, please grant me the power to admit my failing, assume responsibility, change direction, and make amends where needed.

Every man shall bear his own burden.
Galatians 6:5

86

Sometimes, dear God, I take myself way too seriously! That's why I'm coming to You in prayer today asking for the blessing of a **LIGHT SPIRIT** within me. Let me be able to tell the difference between those things that are truly important and those that are not so I may respond to others with kindly humor and gentle, appropriate words.

A soft answer turneth away wrath.
Proverbs 15:1

87

What do I really believe? I ask myself this question over and over as I continue on my spiritual journey. Dear God, open to me the mysteries of belief, faith, and **CONVICTION**. Show me how to embrace You with my entire being, and then live according to Your will and Your way.

Prove all things; hold fast that which is good.
1 Thessalonians 5:21

88

I mix with people of many different faiths, and some with no faith at all. I pray for wisdom in knowing how to speak of spiritual things without giving offense, but to learn from others and to share with them. Teach me, God, the way of **TOLERANCE** that bars no one from the reality of Your love.

Judge not, and ye shall not be judged.
Luke 6:37

89

As I count my blessings, dear God, I realize You have given me great **RICHES**. You have granted me a heart willing and able to hear Your voice, and a mind able to comprehend Your work in my life. You have set for me a good path, God, and for this and all Your blessings I see in my life right now, I thank You.

Be rich in good works.
1 Timothy 6:18

90

I'm bombarded with ads telling me how buying a product will make me feel good about myself, but I know these claims are false. How many times has the glow of an extravagant purchase faded before I even got it home? I thank You, God, for the gift of real **SELF-ESTEEM**... and this is knowing that I am deeply loved and cherished by You.

My kindness shall not depart from thee.
Isaiah 54:10

91

Who are my **ROLE MODELS?** These are the people I admire... the people I would like to be like. For these people I name in my heart, dear God, I pray... And because I realize how much they have influenced me, I ask You to keep me aware of how my words and actions may influence others. May I be the kind of role model You would have me to be!

I have given you an example, that ye should do as I have done to you.
John 13:15

92

Sometimes I have **DOUBTS**, God. I have doubts about my place in the world, about the accuracy of my perceptions, and even about You. Is Your love for me real? Is Your presence something I can depend on? Do I truly belong to You? Dear God, let Your answers to these questions bring me to a fuller and deeper faith in You.

Be not faithless, but believing.
John 20:27

93

Help me, dear God, deal with disappointing results. When things do not turn out the way I had hoped and planned, keep me from anger and frustration. Rather, teach me to **LEARN** from the experience. Help me look back with wiser eyes, see where I could have made better choices, then act on my learning and receive better results in the future.

He delivereth and rescueth.
Daniel 6:27

94

There is someone in my life, dear God, who needs Your comfort and care, Your guidance and direction in life. Please grant me a way I can reach out without intruding... a way I can show I understand without presuming to "fix" things... a way I can **SHINE THE LIGHT** of Your love on this person and offer Your peace.

The dayspring from on high hath visited us, to give light to them that sit in darkness.
Luke 1:78-79

95

When **STRESS** hits me hard, God, I feel at the end of my rope. Too many responsibilities, too many things to do, too many worries! Turn my eyes away from all those things, God, and toward You. Let me rest for awhile in Your presence, then I can return to my day with new eyes... new appreciation... new strength.

The Lord stood with me, and strengthened me.
2 Timothy 4:17

96

Dear God, I know that **SELF-CONTROL** is essential to a life of stability, serenity, and contentment. I pray, therefore, for the ability and willingness to act at all times with moderation and within the boundaries You have set out for me. Show me Your path, and I will walk in Your way.

Let your moderation be known unto all men.
Philippians 4:5

97

I need to get away from the noise and distractions around me, if only for a little time. I need some extra **MOMENTS WITH YOU**, God, without my cell phone ringing or my computer beeping. Can the world exist without my attention while I get some fresh air for my body... for my soul? Help me surrender these things to you, God, and help me draw close to You to find rest.

Draw nigh to God, and he will draw nigh to you.
James 4:8

98

If it were not for my own experience with pain, it would be impossible to **EMPATHIZE** with the pain of others. If it were not for my own knowledge of weakness and temptation, it would be difficult to have compassion on those bound in the chains of human frailties. I never thought I would say this, God, but I do: thank You for the hardships and the troubles I have known.

Rejoice with them that do rejoice,
and weep with them that weep.
Romans 12:15

99

Dear God, when a relationship frays, it's tempting to put all the blame on the other person. How clearly I see their faults! But You ask me to look inside myself and admit my own faults. Why? Because it's Your way of empowering me to start the process of making amends... to enable me to repair and **REWEAVE THE TIES** between one human being and another.

Keep on loving one another as brother and sisters.
Hebrews 13:1 NIV

100 I know how to be a gracious giver, but it's harder for me to be a gracious receiver. Dear God, enable me to lose the false pride that would keep me from asking others for their thoughts and prayers... accepting their offers of help and counsel... receiving their care and concern with thanksgiving. Help me to both give and **RECEIVE** with open arms.

What goodness the LORD shall do unto us,
the same will we do unto thee.
Numbers 10:32

101 It's been a long time since I've felt that good feeling I get after a real authentic **LAUGH**... the kind of laugh, dear God, that You call "medicine." Today, I'll take some time out to throw my head back and laugh... to watch a funny movie... to hear a good joke... to visit a friend who always seems to have a hilarious story to tell. After all, isn't a laugh a day the minimum daily requirement? Thank you, God, for the gift of laughter.

A merry heart doeth good like a medicine.
Proverbs 17:22

102 Many times I've made a list of blessings in my life, and thanked You, God, for every single one. But today I want to do something a little different. I want to focus on **ONE GOOD THING** in particular... one blessing that gives my life its meaning, that fills my life with joy...and offer to You my sincere, heart-deep gratitude.

Offer to God thanksgiving.
Psalm 50:14

103

God, You promise to **HELP** in times of need.
When troubles of any kind come my way, open
my eyes so I will see, recognize, and gladly accept
the help You send... whether physicians, counselors,
ministers... or neighbors, friends, even strangers.
Thank You, God, for all the ways You come to
my aid.

*God is our refuge and strength, a very present
help in trouble.*
        Psalm 46:1

104

It's a question of **PERCEPTION**: Is the glass half
full, or half empty? Dear God, help me avoid the
pitfall of focusing so much on what's wrong that I
fail to see what's right... or so much on my successes
that I neglect my weaknesses. Grant me the ability
to perceive myself and my circumstances with clarity
and courage.

*For now we see through a glass, darkly;
but then face to face.*
        1 Corinthians 13:12

105

God, how do I know You are there? You are
invisible to me! Yet You have made the winds to
sweep across my face, the air to bring life to my
body, and my spirit within to hope, dream, feel,
weep, and rejoice. All these things are invisible,
but present... unseen but existing... **REAL**...
true... just like You.

*God's invisible qualities... have been clearly seen,
being understood from what has been made.*
        Romans 1:20 NIV

106 **YOUTHFULNESS** of body passes with time, because that's the way You created us, God. But You gave us something that can retain its youthfulness, and that is the spirit within us. Despite the passing years, enable me to keep a fresh, vibrant spirit... a heart and mind open to ideas, discoveries, and awe. Keep my spirit, God, forever young!

The light of the eyes rejoiceth the heart.
Proverbs 15:30

107 **CONVENIENCE!** It's a must for products and services that want to attract people on the go. Yet, God, I pray that convenience never becomes so central to my life that I fail to do what needs to be done, even when it's not convenient for me. God, never let convenience stand between me and someone who needs me to listen... to be there... to care.

When he saw him, he had compassion on him.
Luke 10:33

108 Before running out onto the field, athletes stretch. They exercise to get their muscles warmed up so they'll be ready for the big game. Show me, God, how to **STRETCH SPIRITUALLY**. Show me how to exercise myself every day in Your will so I will be ready to respond to others with compassion, gentleness, energy, and love.

Lord, I am ready to go with thee.
Luke 22:33

109

"Tomorrow," I promise myself, "I'll do it tomorrow." You know what happens, God. Tomorrow gets as busy as today, and I put it off again. Teach me a new motto: **DO IT NOW!** Help me stop procrastinating. Pray now... meditate now... do what's important first. Now.

Seek ye the LORD while he may be found,
call ye upon him while he is near.
Isaiah 55:6

110

Sometimes, God, Your voice is clear; but at other times, You speak in a gentle whisper. These are the stirrings of spirit that breathe in silence... the spark of intuition that kindles awareness... the seed of wisdom that grows and matures with faithful listening to You. Empower me, dear God, to **HEAR YOUR VOICE.**

The LORD was not in the fire: and after the fire
a still small voice.
1 Kings 19:12

111

Many have noted, God, that You created us with two ears but only one mouth. I get the message! Grant me the willingness to listen more than I speak; and when I speak, to say neither too much nor too little. Grant me the ability to **SPEAK WISELY**, choosing my words with thoughtfulness and care.

The tongue of the wise useth knowledge aright: but the mouth of fools poureth out foolishness.
Proverbs 15:2

112

You know all things, God... and, no surprise to You, I don't. That's why I'm praying today for **TRUST** in You, especially when trust isn't easy. When bad news comes, when things aren't working out, when the way ahead seems full of barriers and obstacles, help me have confidence in Your power to lead me through to the end.

All things work together for good to them that love God.
Romans 8:28

113

I guess if I could build a wall around my life, I would. But I can't, and sometimes things come into my life that are difficult to handle and impossible to change. Dear God, give me strength to **ADAPT**. Keep me from letting negative influences take away my peace of mind. In Your love, show me how to make the best of every situation.

I have learned, in whatsoever state I am, therewith to be content.
Philippians 4:11

114

I don't want to fight against Your will for me, God. Despite the power of my earnest desires and fondest dreams, enlarge my vision to see Your far greater power. I want to **SURRENDER** all to You, for You alone know what's best for me and those I love. You alone hold the keys to my today, tomorrow, forever.

Not my will, but thine, be done.
Luke 22:42

115

In sports, it's called **"TIME OUT."** I need to call "time out" on myself, God, when my mind fills up with negative thoughts. Thoughts unkind to myself or others... thoughts gloomy and depressing... thoughts impure or frivolous leave no room in my heart for You. Cleanse me, God, so You will be at home in me.

For the word of God... judges the thoughts and attitudes of the heart.
Hebrews 4:12 NIV

116

Problem-solving is an art, and, dear God, I'm not very good at it. Help me evaluate my **PROBLEMS** objectively, and take effective steps toward solutions. Grant me the courage to do what's necessary, along with the willingness to ask for help and advice where needed. Free me, God, from the burden of lingering problems.

Cast thy burden upon the LORD, and he shall sustain thee.
Proverbs 14:10

117

Sometimes my **EMOTIONS** get the best of me. I act impulsively, and then regret what I did. God, help me control my emotions so emotions do not control my life, but enhance my life, as You intend. Please grant me the power to refuse hasty decisions and curb rash actions. Make the gift of my emotions, God, serve me better.

And to knowledge, self-control.
2 Peter 1:6 NIV

118

Dear God, I dream of trying new ideas, going to different places, doing things I've never done before. But, of course, that means getting out of my comfort zone. It means I might find myself lost or not knowing what to do next. But it also means experiencing more of my life and Your awesome creation. Grant me, God, the courage to **BROADEN MY HORIZONS.**

Where you go I will go, and where you stay I will stay.
Ruth 1:16 NIV

119

Life becomes unbalanced so easily. We can get so absorbed in things like the computer, hobbies, even our jobs, that every minute of precious time is consumed. Help me, God, put **BALANCE** in my life where unbalance reigns. Grant me the self-control I need to keep work and play in their proper place so I do not neglect the most important things in life.

Live a life worthy of the calling you have received.
Ephesians 4:1 NIV

120

I want to thank You, God, for the people who share my life. Yet so often I find myself taking them for granted—I expect them to be there for me. I hardly listen to what they are saying to me. Forgive me, God, and grant me the gift of **ATTENTIVENESS** in all my relationships. Help me treat my loved ones as the unique and wonderful blessings they truly are.

In your relationships with one another,
have the same mindset as Christ Jesus.
Philippians 2:5 NIV

121

What's **POSSIBLE?** For You, God, everything is possible. Grant me a heart that yearns for You in my daily life, that seeks to know You better. Enhance my understanding so I will more appreciate the good and true things around me. Help me, God, to be the person I want to be... because, with You, it's completely possible.

With God all things are possible.
Matthew 19:26

122

Self-talk is powerful. If I tell myself over and over that I can't, then I don't even want to try. But, God, if I tell myself repeatedly that You are with me and will help me, then what? There's no limit to what could happen! I pray for **SELF-TALK** that echoes Your loving feelings toward me and Your good will for my life.

For as he thinketh in his heart, so is he.
Proverbs 23:7

123 Teach me, God, to trust in You with all my heart, and not to lean on my own understanding. Help me remember that all things are in Your hands, for there's nothing outside Your power or beyond Your wisdom. Wherever life's path may be taking me and in whatever challenges I am facing today, let me always place complete **RELIANCE** on Your continuing kindness and love.

Trust in him at all times.
Psalm 62:8

124 Too often I lose sight of the blessings You continue to shower on me. Today I want to open my heart in **GRATITUDE** for all the good things I enjoy...for the delight of life, for the presence of my loved ones, and for the wonder of Your creation. Grant me, dear God, a heart of genuine gratitude and praise.

There shall be showers of blessing.
Ezekiel 34:26

125 The world would have me find my self-worth in how much money I make, in where I live, or in what I own. You, dear God, have a different idea! Before I was born, You knew me, and in Your mercy, You made me Your **BELOVED CHILD**. With You, I can be the person You have called me to be... a person deeply loved not because of who I am, but because of *whose* I am.

For everyone belongs to me.
Ezekiel 18:4 NIV

126 Dear God, grant me **PATIENCE** with situations, with others, and with myself. When things aren't going my way, remind me to step back and allow Your way to unfold. When I'm overwhelmed with feelings of frustration, grant me the ability to speak and act with moderation and kindness. Let my patience reflect Your unending patience with me.

The patient in spirit is better than the proud in spirit.
Ecclesiastes 7:8

127 Dear God, I'm always striving to make things happen. I pray, teach me when to **ALLOW** things to happen. Sometimes it's another person's role to take the lead, and mine to offer assistance. Sometimes it's Your desire to show me Your will in Your own way and in Your own time. Enable me, God, to step back and let You get to work!

Cast all your anxiety on him because he cares for you.
1 Peter 5:7 NIV

128 I'm willing to **SHARE** my money when I have extra, and I'll give my time when there's nothing else on my calendar. But God, You would have me go the extra mile... to share with others even when my finances are tight and my time is short. Grant me willingness, dear God, to go the extra mile for others.

And let us not be weary in well doing...
Galatians 6:9

129

I began my spiritual journey as a search for something **BIGGER THAN MYSELF** to believe in... to follow... to love. All this, dear God, I have found in You! I realize my life is incomplete without You, and my heart has no comfort without the presence of Your Spirit. Travel with me, I pray, from this day and all the days of my life.

And my Spirit remains among you.
Haggai 2:5 NIV

130

The **POSSIBILITIES** are endless! How do I know which ones I should pursue and those I should leave behind? I ask You to lead me as I make my day-to-day choices. Guide me especially in those small, everyday choices that so often open doors to big opportunities and meaningful relationships. Yes, there are so many possibilities... direct my path, dear God!

In all thy ways acknowledge him,
and he shall direct thy paths.
Proverbs 3:6

131
Creator-God, You have made the sun and moon, the stars and galaxies, yet You care for the smallest of living things here on earth. With Your example as my guide, I pray for **FAITHFULNESS** in all I do, whether I am called to attempt great things today, or to perform small, common acts of kindness and love.

Whoever can be trusted with very little can also be trusted with much.
Luke 16:10 NIV

132
Lord, guide me as I try to **FOLLOW** You in the things I do and say. Let Your Word open my eyes and ears to Your truth so I may walk the path ahead of me with the light of wisdom that comes only from You. Even though the world around me may choose another direction, keep me close by Your side forever.

Follow me.
Matthew 4:19

133
Dear God, I ask You for the gift of **HEALING**. Grant wholeness of body and spirit to those who suffer, especially the ones I name within my heart. If it is Your will, remove the burden of pain and illness so all may turn to You in joyful thanks and praise.

He healeth the broken in heart,
and bindeth up their wounds.
Psalm 147:3

134

You lovingly invite me, dear God, to come to You in **PRAYER**. What a privilege! Enfold me in the knowledge that You desire to hear my voice. Increase in me, the desire to take my needs, the needs of my loved ones, and the needs of the world to You in heartfelt prayer, believing that You will answer.

Pray without ceasing.
1 Thessalonians 5:17

135

HUMILITY is more than a claim; rather, it's a state of being. That's why, dear God, I want my humility to be more than what I say or imagine I have, but a quality my heart possesses. Turn my thoughts away from competition with others and from measuring myself against them, and toward an acknowledgement that all I have and am comes from You.

Do not think of yourself more highly than you ought.
Romans 12:3 NIV

136

Dear God, please help me **RECONCILE** the gap between what I say and what I do. Remove my tendency to admonish others while giving myself a free pass... to correct the behavior of those around me while imagining my own actions beyond reproach. Yes, there's a big gap sometimes! Help me to act in the way that I require of others.

Why do you look at the speck of sawdust in your brother's eye and pay no attention to the plank in your own eye?
Matthew 7:3 NIV

137

Shall I play it safe or take a **RISK**? So many decisions come down to choosing one of those two options. What about it, God? What should I do? Caution pulls me one way; adventure pulls me another. All I can do right now is thank You, God, for the comfort of knowing that whichever way I go, You will be with me.

My spirit remaineth among you: fear ye not.
Haggai 2:5

138

Dear God, I want to **CONTRIBUTE** more than just money to causes that mean something to me. When I feel drawn to an organization that is making a difference in the world, I want a chance to give of myself. Lead me, God, to the people and places that could use my skills and expertise, and would welcome my help.

Silver or gold I do not have,
but what I do have I give you.
Acts 3:6 NIV

139

Because I hear them spoken all the time by others, vulgar words come out of my mouth, too. I use expressions I don't like, and, dear God, I know You don't like them, either. Forgive me when I say these things. Help me overcome this habit so all my **COMMUNICATION** will be uplifting... meaningful...and most of all, pleasing to You.

But just as he who called you is holy,
so be holy in all you do.
1 Peter 1:15 NIV

140

If it were not for **FAILURE**, dear God, I would never know success. That's easy for me to say, of course—but when failure comes my way, grant me the maturity and wisdom to take it as an occasion to rethink, relearn, and redirect. Be with me at all times, but especially when I feel I have failed.

He who listens to a life-giving rebuke will be
at home among the wise.
Proverbs 15:31 NIV

141 Sometimes, dear God, I put boundaries around myself, limiting myself to familiar and predictable things. Why not do something different today? God, I want to **SURPRISE MYSELF**, maybe by discovering a hidden talent, or reaching out to someone I don't know very well, or developing a needed skill. I want to learn more about Your unique and amazing creation—me!

Who is like you – majestic in holiness,
awesome in glory, working wonders?
Exodus 15:11 NIV

142 **CORE STRENGTH** is what holds houses up and keeps buildings from tumbling down. Core strength, too, is what my spirit needs to keep from crumbling in the face of life's trials and troubles. Spiritual core strength comes from You and for this I ask. I pray that you will live as an unshakable strength in my heart!

It fell not: for it was founded upon a rock.
Matthew 7:25

143

When I see something that needs to get done, dear God, grant me the **INITIATIVE** to do it. Don't let me wait for someone else to come along and take care of it, as I do so often. Instead, put in me the willingness to step forward and, without complaint, take on the project and finish it.

Here am I; send me.
Isaiah 6:8

144

While a good **REPUTATION** takes a long time to build up, it takes only a few seconds to tear down. Impress on me this truth, dear God. Guard my behavior so I gain and keep a good reputation among my family, friends, and associates. Prevent me from doing or saying anything that would unjustly tarnish the reputation of someone else. A good reputation is priceless!

Thou shalt not bear false witness against thy neighbour.
Exodus 20:16

145

Worthwhile goals take **PERSISTENCE**. They require a willingness to work every day... to follow step-to-step rules... to stick with it it, even when little progress is apparent. The spiritual walk is like this, too. I pray, God, to remain persistent in my search for spiritual maturity and a deeper knowledge of You.

I press toward the mark for the prize of the high calling of God in Christ Jesus.
Philippians 3:14

146

What will **RESULT** from what I'm about to do? Dear God, help me pause and ask this question whenever I'm on the brink of a questionable action. Call to my mind the people I might harm, or the damage I might do to myself and my hopes for the future. Help me act on only those things likely to bring about the best possible consequences.

Pray for us: for we trust we have a good conscience, in all things willing to live honestly.
Hebrews 13:18

147

I think I am able to resist **TEMPTATION**, but when it comes, I fall. These times have taught me, God, that I cannot overcome temptation by myself. I know from experience that it takes more than what I have within me to turn away! Please send Your strength into my heart and mind. Grant me self-control over those things that tempt me.

Blessed is the man who perseveres under trial.
James 1:12 NIV

148

I have promised myself that I will conquer my weaknesses. Yet, no matter how strong my resolve, only You can lift the gloom of guilt that hangs over me like a shadow. Only You can release me from the hold of addictions and other oppressors. Only You, God, offer true **DELIVERANCE** that will heal me now and last forever.

He hath sent me to heal the brokenhearted.
Luke 4:18

149

"If all else fails, read the **INSTRUCTIONS**." This humorous piece of advice applies to the spiritual life, too! When my own thoughts prove unsatisfactory and I'm tired of listening to others' opinions, maybe it's time for me to open the scriptures. Let my heart and mind be filled with Your "instructions" for my life, dear God.

All scripture is given by inspiration of God.
2 Timothy 3:16

150

Many authors and motivational speakers claim they have the keys to **SUCCESS**, but what do they mean by success? Most of the time, God, it's not the kind of success You talk about. Your success isn't so much about getting, but about giving...not so much about striving, but about being. God, grant me Your kind of success in my life.

He holds success in store for the upright.
Proverbs 2:7 NIV

151 **RESENTMENT** clings to me, and I can't seem to shake it off. Please grant me, God, the spiritual maturity I need to let go of old grudges and sour memories. Allow me the ability to forgive myself and others from the heart so bitterness will no longer shadow my thoughts. Free me, God, from the dust of the past.

Get rid of all bitterness, rage and anger.
Ephesians 4:31 NIV

152 There's a place in my **HEART**, God, that only You can fill. Remove from me anything that stands in Your place. Banish chaos from the outside world and chatter from my own thoughts from the stillness within. Provide me with an urgent desire to make sure my heart remains a pleasing place for You.

Mercy unto you, and peace, and love, be multiplied.
Jude 1:2

153 Thank You, God, for the power of prayer. Help me **PRAY** regularly and with attentiveness, asking You in faith for all that I need and desire. Teach me to pray for all things according to Your will.

Ask, and ye shall receive, that your joy may be full.
John 16:24

154

Dear God, please grant me **WELLNESS** of body and mind. As much as it is within my power, let me take the steps necessary to reach the healthfulness you desire for me. If You see fit to let a certain physical or emotional weakness remain, let me accept it with contentment and grace.

The fear of the LORD leads to life; then one rests content, untouched by trouble.
Proverbs 19:23 NIV

155

Many times, people know the **TRUTH**, but would rather turn away. I know that happens with me, dear God, when the truth is uncomfortable, difficult, or troublesome. That's why I'm coming to You in prayer today asking for the courage to face the truth in all circumstances, especially those You most desire for me to hear.

Ye shall know the truth, and the truth shall make you free.
John 8:32

156

It has been found many times that we human beings are more alike than different. When I'm tempted to separate people into "us" and "them" in thought, word, or action, God, help me stop and think about what I'm doing. Remind me of our **ONENESS**... the unity that makes us all Your creation and your children.

Have we not all one father? hath not one God created us?
Malachi 2:10

157 The value of voluntary **SERVICE** to others is becoming more and more appreciated. Helpful, generous, willing service has been one of the hallmarks of Your people for generations, and it still is. Grant me, dear God, hands and heart dedicated to service wherever I may be.

Freely ye have received, freely give.
Matthew 10:8

158 When I *believe* there's **PLENTY**, God, I discover there *is* plenty. I find I have what I need to get by today without worrying about tomorrow. I discover satisfaction in what I have without giving a thought to what I'm missing. When I live with my heart and mind directed toward you, God, I possess more than enough.

For as he thinketh in his heart, so is he.
Proverbs 23:7

159 Because I'm so conscious of my weaknesses and failings, God, I'm easily intimidated. Help me get rid of these feelings! In their place, provide me with the inner strength and confidence I need to be able to **BELIEVE IN MYSELF**. Remind me, especially when I'm feeling ill at ease with others, of Your continuing love and strong presence in my life.

If God be for us, who can be against us?
Romans 8:31

160

I've learned this from experience: not every gadget that promises to make my life easier lives up to its promise. **YOUR PROMISES**, however, are different. You promise to lighten the burdens of my heart...You promise to ease the weight of life's trials...You promise to keep me in Your love forever. Your promises, God, make my life much easier!

The Lord is not slack concerning his promise.
2 Peter 3:9

161

When I see someone I love going down the wrong path, I want to **INTERVENE**. How can I best do this, God? Please help me find the right time and the right words to open a conversation about my care and concern. Grant me the ability to listen, seeking not to force my own solution, but to help my loved one initiate needed changes.

He that handleth a matter wisely shall find good:
and whoso trusteth in the LORD, happy is he.
Proverbs 16:20

162 You assure me of Your protection, God, but Your promise doesn't free me from addressing my personal **SAFETY**. Keep me alert to danger signs as I go about the business of my day, and grant me the willingness to take reasonable precautions when I am at home and when I am out. Keep me and my loved ones safe in Your care.

He shall cover thee with his feathers,
and under his wings shalt thou trust.
Psalm 91:4

163 People who are blessed to have healthy and stable **FRIENDSHIPS** are happy people, and I certainly understand why. Friends share our joys and griefs, our milestones and celebrations. Friends support, encourage, help, care, and love. Thank You, dear God, for the friends I name in my heart today!

I have called you friends.
John 15:15

164

"Let your **CONSCIENCE** be your guide," the saying goes. But is it a reliable guide? Not if I have muffled its voice by justifying wrong actions and conduct. Clear my conscience, dear God, of anything that would divert my path from You. Fill my heart with the desire to follow Your will... and then when my conscience is my guide, it will lead me straight to You.

We trust we have a good conscience,
in all things willing to live honestly.
Hebrews 13:18

165

When my habits and routines dull my awareness of You, **AWAKEN** my spirit. Touch my heart and make me alive to Your presence in my life, to the blessings You have provided to me, and to the miracles all around me. When my inner life lies dormant, God, let the light of Your love shine on me.

My voice shalt thou hear in the morning, O LORD;
in the morning will I direct my prayer unto thee,
and will look up."
Psalm 5:3

166 **ONE DAY AT A TIME!** Sometimes I hardly remember what I did today because I was so busy reliving, rehashing, regretting what I did yesterday... so busy thinking, worrying, stressing about tomorrow. Let me take my days, God, the same way You give them to me—one at a time.

And the evening and the morning were the first day.
Genesis 1:5

167 More and more I hear about the physical and spiritual benefits of walking. Fresh air refreshes body and mind, and exercise loosens tight muscles and relaxes tension. And what better way to see and appreciate Your **CREATION**, God? Today, open the wonders of Your creation to me!

God saw every thing that he had made,
and, behold, it was very good.
Genesis 1:31

168 When things aren't going smoothly, being **POSITIVE** is a challenge. But I want to meet the challenge of staying positive in the face of negative circumstances, dear God, and I know I can with Your help. Remind me of Your strength and power within me, and tell me again about Your good plans for me. May temporary set-backs serve to draw me closer to You in trust and love.

I was brought low, and he helped me.
Psalm 116:6

169

How I respond to real or perceived slights tells me a lot about myself. For those times I lash out in anger, dear God, forgive me. Help me more easily take control of my **REACTIONS** when I feel threatened. Only by controlling myself can I keep a cool head in every circumstance.

He that is slow to wrath is of great understanding.
Proverbs 14:29

170

Happiness comes from the ability to find **ENJOYMENT** in everyday pleasures. Grant me the ability, dear God, to delight myself in simple things... in being alone with a good book... in sharing amiable companionship with others... in watering a blooming flower... in petting a furry friend. In these, let me take my joy!

This is the day which the Lord hath made;
we will rejoice and be glad in it.
Psalm 118:24

171

Doing what's **RIGHT** might not always come easy, but it's what I want to do. Dear God, I want to be the one who chooses what's right, even when it's not the most popular choice. I desire to continue doing what's right, even if others have abandoned the cause. I need Your strength, God, because I know I can do it with You.

What doth the LORD require of thee, but to do justly, and to love mercy, and to walk humbly with thy God?
Micah 6:8

172

Do I schedule time for **MEDITATION?** As I work on nurturing my spiritual life, dear God, I want to make sure I have at least a few minutes every day to rest quietly in thought with You. From now on, God, I'm making a date each day with You... and I plan to keep it.

*I will meditate in thy precepts,
and have respect unto thy ways.*
Psalm 119:15

173

I must live with **UNCERTAINTIES** at times. As much as I would like to have definitive answers to questions that concern me right now, I know I'm not going to get them... at least not yet. Help me, God, to wait until reliable and truthful solutions arise; and meanwhile, keep me calm in the midst of uncertainties.

God is not the author of confusion, but of peace.
1 Corinthians 14:33

174 People say that we're unable to pay attention to any one topic for more than a few minutes! Yes, distractions all around us can take our eyes, ears, and heart away from what's important to see, hear, and understand. Grant me the gift of **CONCENTRATION**, most especially attentiveness to your faith-filled path.

Lord, what wait I for? my hope is in thee.
Psalm 39:7

175 Dear God, You ask for **PERFECTION**, but not perfectionism. As I grasp frantically for some impossible earthly goal, I miss the perfection You offer me... the perfection of Your love. You give of Yourself, embracing me in Your care, wrapping me in the peace You alone possess.

Be perfect, therefore, as your heavenly Father is perfect.
Matthew 5:48 NIV

176 Help me remember, God, to **BREATHE DEEPLY**. No, not just when I'm frustrated or angry; but any time. Let me consciously and attentively breathe in the good fresh air as I absorb the fullness of Your love for me. And as I exhale, let gratitude flow from my heart, acknowledging all the blessings You are providing for me in that very moment.

O give thanks unto the LORD; for he is good.
Psalm 118:1

177 Whoops! I did it again... and now I want to beat myself up about it. Grant me the self-acceptance I need, God, to keep my **MISTAKES** in perspective. Help me be as forgiving to myself as I am to others... as tolerant with my own weaknesses as I am of the weaknesses of others. Forgive me, God, and help me move on!

Have mercy upon me, O LORD; for I am weak.
Psalm 6:2

178 How long has it been since I've shown my loved ones how much they mean to me? I say the words... but I rarely make a point of doing something special just for them not because it's their birthday, but just because I love them. God, today let my **AFFECTION** for others be reflected in my actions!

Let us not love in word, neither in tongue;
but in deed and in truth.
1 John 3:18

179 It's been noted that if we aren't happy right where we are, we won't be happy anyplace else. How true! Teach me, dear God, the art of **HAPPINESS** that surpasses my circumstances and the moods of those around me. And I know what will happen: suddenly, things won't look so dreary... and I'll discover happiness wherever You see fit to put me!

Rejoice, because your names are written in heaven.
Luke 10:20

180 My ability to **BOUNCE BACK** after failure will help me keep going forward with energy and vitality. It's a matter of pressing on, even though my feelings may lag behind. Please grant me the willingness and desire to move forward, ready to embrace new challenges and new opportunities as they open to me.

Let us run with patience the race that is set before us.
Hebrews 12:1

181 Who's in **CONTROL?** I like to think I am, God, but I know it's not true. All the proof I need comes in the shape of unexpected events—I have no control over them. All the proof I need gets right in my face when sickness flattens me, when a sure-thing crumbles, when reality hits me on the side of the head. Who's in control? I know: You.

Truly my soul waiteth upon God...
He only is my rock and my salvation.
Psalm 62:1

182 God, You offer Yourself as my constant and perfect **MENTOR**. You were born to show me how to live, and to teach me the ways of holiness and truth. Everyone needs someone to go ahead, to set an example, to light the way... and for me, God, that "someone" is You.

I am the way, the truth, and the life.
John 14:6

183 When I'm full of myself, thinking my own thoughts, making my own plans, reveling in my own imagined future... as You can see, God, I'm not thinking much about You or anyone else. How could I? There's no room left! God, help me get rid of self-congratulating **PRIDE**; help me make room in my heart for You.

God resisteth the proud, and giveth grace to the humble.
1 Peter 5:5

184 Dear God, I'm not the person I want to be... and I can't seem to get out of the grip of self-pity. I pout. I cry. What can I do? I can come to You, God, knowing that You love me regardless of my appearance, my mistakes, my status in life. Your love pulls me up from the pit... and in Your love, I'll learn to love myself, **JUST AS I AM**.

By the grace of God I am what I am.
1 Corinthians 15:10

185

I'd like to put on a positive, faith-filled attitude the same way I put on a shirt...just slide it over me and wear it for the rest of the day. Can I do that, dear God? Through your Word, I hear you say "yes." All I need to do is take off my anger, my bitterness, my self-importance... then humble my heart and **CLOTHE MYSELF** in Your overwhelming love.

Therefore, as God's chosen people, holy and dearly loved, clothe yourselves with compassion, kindness, humility, gentleness and patience.
Colossians 3:12 NIV

186

Dear God, I desire to heighten the experience of life. **ENRICH** my days, I pray, with a deeper understanding of my life's purpose and a genuine commitment to Your ways and Your values. Broaden my vision of life so I may see it as more than simply survival, but as the beautiful adventure You created it to be.

"For I know the plans I have for you," declares the LORD, "plans to prosper you and not to harm you, plans to give you hope and a future."
Jeremiah 29:11 NIV

187

As You **CARE** for me, dear God, increase my readiness to care for others. Grant me the patience it takes to truly understand the needs of those around me, and the willingness to respond to them with real and practical help. I want to show I care, even if it means going out of my way... even if it means taking time out for them.

As we have therefore opportunity,
let us do good unto all men.
Galatians 6:10

188

Many people talk about **FREEDOM**, but only a few take practical steps to defend it. Help me, dear God, be one of those few. Let me embrace not only freedom, but the responsibilities that go with it. And, God, grant me the grace to realize that true and lasting freedom comes from knowing You.

Where the Spirit of the Lord is,
there is liberty.
2 Corinthians 3:17

189 When I really need someone's help or advice, there are only a few I call on... the few who I know will respond, no matter what. Dear God, I want to make sure that I'LL BE THERE for them, too. Let me never forget how much they have helped me out in the past... let me never fail to respond when I can be their source of comfort and guidance.

By love serve one another.
Galatians 5:13

190 Days fly by as I find myself running from one URGENT request to another. My life is jam-packed with "musts," "shoulds" and "have to's"! Help me sort it all out, God. Show me a better way to live... a more realistic perspective... a wiser set of priorities. Let me live each day, God, knowing what's truly important.

What is seen is temporary,
but what is unseen is eternal.
2 Corinthians 4:18 NIV

191

PRACTICE, practice, practice! That's what it takes to be good at anything. I'm coming to realize that the same is true in spiritual life, too. I pray, dear God, that You would grant me the motivation to practice being the kind of person You invite me to be. Let me never get tired of taking time out for You, for learning and listening to your Word, and of passing along Your love to others.

He that overcometh shall inherit all things.
Revelation 21:7

192

Thank you, dear God, for the gift of my dreams and goals. Now, please grant me the will and desire I need to **ACHIEVE** them. True achievement takes work and motivation... the ability to hold on when the going gets rough... the belief, deep within, that this dream can come true. God, lead me toward genuine achievement.

The desire accomplished is sweet to the soul.
Proverbs 13:19

193

Dear God, there are times when I need to **FOLLOW MY HEART**... times when, to other people, what I'm doing may seem odd. When I come to You in prayer about these matters, God, grant me clarity and courage. No matter what the future may bring, after seeking Your will and guidance, help me to be true to myself and follow my heart.

Let us search and try our ways,
and turn again to the LORD.
Lamentations 3:40

194

There's so much danger in the world, dear God! The stories I hear and the day's main headlines all tell of threats and counter-threats among nations, chaos and upheavals across the globe. That's why, God, I pray for the strength and courage it takes not to **WORRY**, but to put my time and energy to work for peace... to rely on You in all situations... and to pray.

Can any one of you by worrying add a single hour
to your life?
Matthew 6:27 NIV

195 Today I pray, dear God, for the **SPIRITUAL AWARENESS** of those I love. Open their eyes to their blessings, and plant in them a heart of gratitude to You. Touch the lives of my loved ones, God, so they can know Your comfort and care, and most especially, Your never-ending love for them, no matter what they have done or where they are. Let them open their lives to You.

The LORD watches over all who love him.
Psalm 145:20 NIV

196 God, grant me the grace of physical and spiritual **WELL-BEING**. Though I may deal with certain weaknesses of body or mind, don't let these things define my life. Instead, dear God, inspire me to grab hold of the depth of Your love and compassion for me, and strengthen me with peace of mind that comes only from You.

Let the peace of God rule in your hearts.
Colossians 3:15

197 They say **CIVILITY** is hard to come by these days, and I believe it's true. But what about me? Where could I show more courtesy to others? When do I tend to push others aside or speak without consideration for another's feelings? Dear God, please show me where my words and actions could become more civil.

Be ye kind one to another.
Ephesians 4:32

198

The world defines **MORALITY** one way, dear God, but it isn't always Your way. Help me commit myself to doing what You truly want me to do, even if it's difficult because of what others are doing... or what the world says is OK... or what would be easiest. Grant me the blessing that comes with accepting Your standards for what is right.

As the heavens are higher than the earth, so are my ways higher than your ways and my thoughts than your thoughts.
Isaiah 55:9

199

How do I meet **CHALLENGES?** The only way, I know, is to tackle them head-on. But that takes courage, dear God, and for this I pray. When challenges come my way, grant me the wisdom to overcome them with confidence in my ability to solve problems... with support from others...with trust in Your help... with perseverance and prayer.

We also rejoice in our sufferings, because we know that suffering produces perseverance; perseverance, character; and character, hope.
Romans 5:3-4 NIV

200

An oak tree grows slowly, but when it's mature, it's strong. Its branches are able to withstand the winds and storms of time because its roots extend far into the ground. Dear God, plant the seed of faith in me, and grant me the patience and willingness to let it grow slowly, ever deeper... ever stronger. Let me gradually **INCREASE** in faith.

He shall be like a tree planted by the rivers of water.
Psalm 1:3

201

Dear God, when I'm tempted to act like someone I'm not... to play a part... to wear a mask in front of people... please, God, grant me the courage to be **TRUE TO MYSELF**. I have no reason to fool others, or to try to impress people by being someone I'm not. Let me live in authenticity, God, and I will never be ashamed to be who I really am.

Let me not be ashamed; for I put my trust in thee.
Psalm 25:20

202

I TREASURE LIFE because You, God, created it. Yet so many faces betray weariness and anguish, despondency and despair. For so many people I meet in the course of my day, life is a heavy burden. Let me be aware when there is an opportunity, God, to show someone the wonder of his or her own life.

An anxious heart weighs a man down,
but a kind word cheers him up.
Proverb 12:25 NIV

203

Typically, we harbor high **IDEALS** when we're young...but as we grow older, those ideals fade. We get cynical and world-weary. Dear God, help me avoid this downward spiral. Let the ideals of my youth change and grow with maturity and experience, yet never let me doubt the attainability of noble goals.

Fight the good fight of faith.
1 Timothy 6:12

204

Dear God, grant me **DEDICATION** to an effort or a cause larger than myself. Enable me to continue my efforts from start to finish, even when it seems I'm making little progress. If the cause is good, God, let my presence and my contributions make a positive difference.

I have fought a good fight,
I have finished my course,
I have kept the faith.
2 Timothy 4:7

205

For what am I willing to **STRIVE?** God, let it be not for money, status, or fame. Why? Because all these things are like shadows that disappear in the light of day. Rather, let me work hard for gifts of the truly meaningful kind, like love, humility, and a servant's heart. These things, dear God, will last a lifetime.

Desire spiritual gifts.
1 Corinthians 14:1

206

Sing! Dance! Love, laugh, **HAVE FUN!** What's stopping me, dear God, from enjoying the life You have given me? What holds me back from embracing all the wonders of this world You have created? Remove needless hindrances, and let me give myself a chance to experience genuine fun today.

No one will take away your joy.
John 16:22 NIV

207

How I'm spending my **MONEY** says a great deal about how I'm spending my life. Am I wasting both on useless things and shallow entertainments, or am I spending my time on worthy goals and things that make life better for myself and others? As I look through my checkbook, God, help me consider how I am spending my money...and my life.

Keep your lives free from the love of money and be content with what you have.
Hebrews 13:5 NIV

208

Sometimes I bite off more than I can chew. I wish I hadn't made that promise...taken on that project... said "yes" when I should have said "maybe" or "no." Now what can I do? God, help me admit my mistake, and then enable me to do everything within my power to **PUT THINGS RIGHT.**

Suppose one of you wants to build a tower. Won't you first sit down and estimate the cost to see if you have enough money to complete it?
Luke 14:28 NIV

209 **DISCIPLINE** may seem old-fashioned but it still has meaning today. God, I need discipline to free myself of bad habits and addictions. In those areas of my life where it's my responsibility to provide discipline to others, give me guidance to help them be the best they can be. Grant me wisdom in areas of discipline so I can grow strong in Your ways.

Correct, rebuke and encourage – with great patience and careful instruction.
2 Timothy 4:2 NIV

210 I often think of my loved ones, and I'm **CONCERNED** about their well-being and happiness. I have many ways I can reach out to them... I can speak to them, listen to what they say, call them or drop them an E-mail... anything to turn my thoughts into action. Today, God, let me show someone how much I care.

Encourage one another daily.
Hebrews 3:13 NIV

211 Thank You, God, for good people...those people who seem to be there at just the right time with a smile and a helping hand, with words of encouragement and a pat on the back. Now I want to pass it on. God, I pray that I can bless others with that kind of **GOODNESS**. Let me be the one to put the good in someone's bad day.

Build each other up.
1 Thessalonians 5:11 NIV

212 Certain people more than try my patience! Teach me, dear God, to realize I have neither the power nor the authority to **CHANGE** anyone, but You can change my heart. Bless these I name, and help me treat them with respect and kindness, and with consideration for their needs and feelings.

Be patient, bearing with one another in love.
Ephesians 4:2 NIV

213 When did doing "random acts of **KINDNESS**" lose its popularity? Certainly not because there are no more acts of kindness left to be done! Please, God, don't let me forget about doing a kindness for others for no other reason than... just because they're there... just because I can.

But those who plan what is good find love and faithfulness.
Proverbs 14:22 NIV

214

Dear God, help me have **FAITH** that everything will turn out all right. Right now I'm not sure which way I should go, and there are some things in my life I'm concerned about. Today I'm looking to You for assurance, and I'm leaning on You for strength and understanding.

According to your faith be it unto you.
Matthew 9:29

215

Dear God, please grant me **DISCERNMENT**. Enable me to think critically about the events of the world so I may form intelligent judgments and provide thoughtful comments. When others are disturbed or distressed, help me give them the assurance, God, of knowing everything in our community, our nation, and our world is in Your hands.

Give your servant a discerning heart.
1 Kings 3:9 NIV

216

What a delicious tidbit it was, dear God! But I'm not talking about food; rather, I'm talking about **GOSSIP**. I'm often so excited to spread it that I forget the power of my words to stab another's heart. I may thoughtlessly carry a story, neglecting to find out if the story is true. God, help me to guard my words with integrity today.

Without wood a fire goes out; without a gossip a quarrel dies down.
Proverbs 26:20 NIV

217 "A STITCH IN TIME saves nine," the saying goes. Today, God, let me pay attention to those things that need doing...those things so easy to put off until they become emergencies. Maybe it's a visit to a health professional. Maybe it's a job around the house. Maybe it's making a realistic budget. Whatever it is, God, let me "save nine" today.

As the Lord hath called every one, so let him walk.
1 Corinthians 7:17

218 We're influenced by—and identified by—the FRIENDS we keep. That's why You would have us pick our friends wisely. Grant me, God, the gift of good and faithful companions. Together, let us encourage and support each other... let us help each other grow in faith and trust in You.

He that walketh with wise men shall be wise.
Proverbs 13:20

219 In a choir, HARMONY happens when sections of the choir complement and support one another. The result is pleasant to hear. In the same way, God, please bless Your people so we may all live together in true harmony. Let our differences come together to create understanding and acceptance in a way that is pleasing to You.

Be likeminded, having the same love,
being of one accord, of one mind.
Philippians 2:2

220 Dear God, grant me the gift of **ENTHUSIASM**, because without it, boredom saps my energy. Help me find excitement in what I'm doing, and let my passion bring satisfaction and fulfillment to my life. To remain enthusiastic is to stay both interested and interesting, no matter where I am or how old I am!

Serve the LORD your God with all your heart and with all your soul.
Deuteronomy 10:12 NIV

221 Dear God, grant me the skills and expertise I need to make my efforts **EFFECTIVE**. Put people in my life from whom I can watch and learn... people to coach me and show me how to achieve the best results. Let me be inspired by those who are effective to learn how to be effective myself.

A great door for effective work has opened to me.
1 Corinthians 16:9 NIV

222 Instead of noticing their faults, God, help me **SEE THE BEST** in others. Let me play up their good qualities... identify the kind things they say and do... compliment their traits that make them special to me and to their loved ones. Let me be willing to describe them as I would want others to describe me.

Judge not, that ye be not judged.
Matthew 7:1

223 "One step forward, two steps back" describes my spiritual experience. I make **PROGRESS**, then I fall back; then I get up and begin again... but I'm a little bit further ahead... a little wiser, a little more experienced... than before. My progress seems so slow, but I ask for Your help to continue on... one step forward... two steps back... another step forward in faith and love.

You need to persevere.
Hebrews 10:36 NIV

224 In continuing love, You hold out to me the gift of getting to know You better. Why do I hold back? What am I waiting for? Dear God, give me the courage to **TAKE A CHANCE** on You. Let me open my arms to receive You, and to discover Your presence in my life.

Believe in God.
John 14:1 NIV

225 I live in community with others, and my words and actions **INFLUENCE** them. God, make me aware of anything I might be doing to lead someone else in the wrong direction... any negative mindset of mine that would persuade another person to adopt a similar attitude. Where I have influence, let it be for the good of those around me.

Lead me in thy truth, and teach me.
Psalm 25:5

226 So often I'm reluctant to **EMPOWER OTHERS**. I'm afraid they won't do the task the same way I would... that it won't be done "right." Yet You empower people, giving us work to do in Your name! I know not everything gets done exactly as You would desire; but You give us the privilege anyway. Dear God, grant me the willingness to allow the same with others.

How good and how pleasant it is for brethren to dwell together in unity!
Psalm 133:1

227 Dear God, I want to know myself so I can reach out to others with true affection. I desire to respond to others not from behind the facade of someone calculated to impress them, but from the heart of who I really am. Let me be genuine with others, remembering who I am- someone completely **LOVED** by You.

I have loved thee with an everlasting love.
Jeremiah 31:3

228 A heart immersed in gratitude is the key to happiness. My heart, therefore, counts blessings... looks on the bright side of things and refuses to get caught up in cynical points of view. Wrap my heart in **THANKFULNESS**, dear God, let me embrace true happiness.

Rejoice in every good thing which the LORD thy God hath given unto thee, and unto thine house.
Deuteronomy 26:11

229 I want to **BELIEVE**, dear God. I want to believe in the higher things, like dreams and ideals...values and principles. I want to believe that my life has meaning and purpose... that through You, I will learn inner wisdom and grace. God, help me to believe in You with all my heart.

I do believe; help me overcome my unbelief!
Mark 9:24 NIV

250 "Those who can laugh at themselves," it is said, "never run out of things to laugh at." Dear God, grant me the ability to **LAUGH AT MYSELF**, especially when I make a silly mistake in front of others. Let me lose my self-consciousness... and welcome the laughter of those who laugh with me.

God has brought me laughter, and everyone who hears about this will laugh with me.
Genesis 21:6 NIV

231 When **DARK DAYS** come, dear God, let the light of Your love shine on me. Rather than dwell on my feelings, help me to focus on the needs of others, because it is in caring for others that we best care for ourselves. Little by little, darkness will pass... things will be brighter again.

God is light, and in him is no darkness at all.
1 John 1:5

232 I feel better about myself when I use **RESTRAINT** in my eating and drinking. Not only do I safeguard my health and well-being, but I serve as an example for others to follow. When I'm tempted to over-do it, God, enable me to restrain myself... for my benefit and the benefit of others.

I am saying this for your own good, not to restrict you, but that you may live in a right way in undivided devotion to the Lord.
1 Corinthians 7:35 NIV

233 I need help to **OVERCOME THE PAST,** dear God. Certain things that have happened in my life continue to trouble my mind and heart. To this day, they affect my thinking and my relationships. Grant me, God, the ability to let go of the past... to say a final good-bye... to leave it behind forever. With Your guidance, help me move forward.

Have mercy upon me, O LORD; for I am weak.
Psalm 6:2

234 When I think I can't, that's when I need to **TRY**. Dear God, give me the motivation I need to take one step up from the one I have reached... to walk one more block... to swim one more lap... to go just a little bit farther. With Your help, all it takes is the willingness to try.

God hath power to help.
2 Chronicles 25:8

235 Though many things and experiences promise **FULFILLMENT**, nothing brings genuine fulfillment in life but You, God. Unlike things of this world, You never change...You are all in all... You satisfy my deepest desires. Fill my heart, dear God, with You.

I am Alpha and Omega, the beginning and the end, the first and the last.
Revelation 22:13

236 As long as I have You, dear God, I'm never **ALONE**. Wherever I am on my life's journey, You are there beside me. Even if I'm walking along the wrong path, You take my hand to guide me back where I need to be. Thank You, God, for the comfort of knowing I'm never alone!

The LORD is nigh unto all them that call upon him.
Psalm 145:18

237 One of the most devastating feelings I can imagine is thinking I have no **PURPOSE IN LIFE**. That's why it means so much to me, God, to know Your will and Your way. Please give me the assurance that no matter what happens, there is ultimate meaning and a divine purpose to everything.

The LORD hath made all things for himself.
Proverbs 16:4

238 When there is an opportunity to do good, dear God, let me be quick to respond. Don't let my natural **HESITATION** keep my hands from reaching out to someone in need, or my feet from running to the aid of others. Instead, I want to be the one others can depend on to be there for them... the same way You are always there for me.

Be not afraid.
Joshua 1:9

239 Like eveyone else, I have a way I like to do things. Sometimes, though, I need to be **FLEXIBLE**. For the sake of another's comfort or pleasure... for the sake of harmony among people... dear God, let me be the one who's willing to do things differently.

Live in harmony with one another.
Romans 12:16 NIV

240 Dear God, help me watch my **MOUTH**. When I'm tempted to say something I shouldn't, grant me the self-control I need to swallow my words rather than speak them aloud. Before I start talking, God, remind me of these three questions: Is it true? Is it kind? Is it necessary?

If anyone considers himself religious and yet does not keep a tight rein on his tongue, he deceives himself and his religion is worthless.
James 1:26 NIV

241

Keep me **SAFE**, dear God, as I go about the activities of my day. Guard me from anything that would hurt or injure me, not only physically, but emotionally and mentally, as well. Protect me from thoughts and imaginings that would harm my relationship with You and hinder my growth in faith.

The Lord shall deliver me from every evil work, and will preserve me unto his heavenly kingdom.
2 Timothy 4:18

242

Where there are rifts in relationships, there are angry words and hurt feelings... turbulent thoughts and stony silences. Help me mend my torn relationships, dear God, by being willing to set aside false pride and **RECONCILE** with the other person. Let me be the one to step forward with an outstretched hand and forgiving heart today.

Do not let the sun go down while you are still angry.
Ephesians 4:26 NIV

243

Many people aspire to stardom. They devise ways to appear on TV and get their names and faces widely recognized. Yet the real **STARS** are those who do Your will and serve their communities. This is the kind of stardom I aspire to, dear God... make me a star that will shine forever.

Each one should use whatever gift he has received to serve others.
1 Peter 4:10 NIV

244 I ask for Your **MERCY**, dear God, when I come before You with my weaknesses and pain. See where I hurt, and touch me with Your healing hand. See where I have gone wrong, and set me on the right path again. I pray for Your mercy, because You are a merciful God.

The LORD thy God is a merciful God.
Deuteronomy 4:31

245 You have intended each one of us to be actively **ENGAGED** in our family, community, and world. Can I lead people? Then let me lead wisely. Can I follow? Then let me follow faithfully. Can I pray? Then let me pray fervently and with a believing heart. Never let me slip into the lie that there is nothing I can do, dear God!

Do those things that are pleasing in his sight.
1 John 3:22

246 Sometimes my thoughts are so jumbled that I can't find the words to explain my feelings! I feel anxious and confused inside. Yet I know, God, that You are the source of **INNER PEACE**. Today please let me receive this gift from You... the gift of quiet thoughts, a calm spirit, and a tranquil heart.

His soul shall dwell at ease.
Psalm 25:13

247 Dear God, grant me the **ENERGY** I need to meet all my responsibilities today. Keep me away from unhealthy habits and frivolous activities that merely deplete my energy and leave me little satisfaction or fulfillment. This day is a gift from You and I pray that I have the energy to use it wisely and enjoy it to the fullest.

Take heed to thyself, and keep thy soul diligently.
Deuteronomy 4:9

248 Dear God, help me sort out the many yearnings of my heart. Provide me with the wisdom I need to clarify and prioritize my goals, and grant me commitment to the path you would have me follow. In all things, I want to reach out and **ASK** in confidence, never doubting Your power to grant my deepest desires.

If ye shall ask any thing in my name, I will do it.
John 14:14

249

Your traits, Your characteristics, and Your power are beyond my **IMAGINATION**, God! No matter how long I meditate on You, I will never fathom the depths of Your wisdom... I will never reach the heights of Your love. Let me rest in what You have given me to know about You, and have joy in the understanding you grant me.

I am the Almighty God.
Genesis 17:1

250

When someone I love has a problem in a relationship, my first inclination is to step in and take sides. Yet, I realize this is **INTERFERING**... this is going where I do not belong. Help me, dear God, remain silent, but supportive... restrained, but there for my loved ones as they work things out together.

If it is to encourage, then give encouragement.
Romans 12:8 NIV

251

GRIEF fills my heart, dear God, to see so many hurting people in the world. I know this grieves You, too, God. Let me bring Your comfort to others whenever I have the opportunity. If I can dry one tear today, God, my day will be complete!

Comfort ye my people, saith your God.
Isaiah 40:1

252 Today, dear God, let me spend my time with You in quiet **CONTEMPLATION**. Point my eyes toward one of Your marvelous works, such as the stars in the sky or a flower at my feet. Turn my thoughts to one of Your attributes, such as Your love and compassion, or Your power and strength. Let my time of contemplation bring me closer to You.

Give ear to my words, O LORD,
consider my meditation.
　　　　Psalm 5:1

253 When I meet someone for the first time, I want to make a good **IMPRESSION**. I want the person to see me as someone who's competent and articulate... caring and kind. Help me, dear God, remember the basics of meeting people—look, smile, shake hands, and greet them as another of Your children, so loved by You.

Greet one another with a kiss of love.
　　　　1 Peter 5:14 NIV

254 **SELFLESSNESS** is about putting others ahead of myself. It means looking back and slowing down for the person lagging behind... about not needing to please myself all the time... about not contriving to be first in every line. Dear God, today send me an opportunity to make one selfless gesture.

Even Christ pleased not himself.
　　　　Romans 15:3

255 I know from experience that when one door closes, another **OPENS**. Yet it takes turning away from the closed door and willingness on my part to look around and find what's open. Dear God, please do this for me: grant me clear eyes and an open mind to discover new opportunities in my life today.

If any man hear my voice, and open the door,
I will come in to him.
Revelation 3:20

256 When hardship or **WEARINESS** threatens to dampen my attitude, dear God, help me stay positive. Let me lessen tension and ease fears so everyone around me can come through a difficult time with grace and dignity. Keep my heart and mind directed toward You and on the needs and comfort of those around me.

Let us not be weary in well doing.
Galatians 6:9

257 It takes more muscles to frown than to **SMILE!** So why don't I smile more often? A simple smile can brighten someone's day... smooth a rough moment... deflect angry words... and lighten my own heart. Dear God, today let me remember to bring the gift of a smile to someone else!

A merry heart maketh a cheerful countenance.
Proverbs 15:13

258 A positive **SELF-CONCEPT** provides me with the ability to manage my circumstances well. I'm aware of my strengths, but I'm not afraid to admit my limitations. I'm confident in myself, but not arrogant in action or attitude. I'm realistic, but still able to believe in my dreams. Dear God, help me keep this positive self-concept as I remember that I am wonderfully made, and deeply loved, by You.

We love him, because he first loved us.
1 John 4:19

259 Dear God, let your presence **WARM** my heart today. Spark the flame of love in me as I reach out to others in word and action. Let the warmth of my kindness and gentleness ease the chill of hatred and anger, always drawing closer to You.

Let us also walk in the Spirit.
Galatians 5:25

260 Every stage of **LIFE** has its challenges... and its triumphs. No matter how old or young we are in years, there are new joys awaiting our discovery. What about me, God? What is it I can do, understand, or accomplish right now that I can at no other time in my life? I pray, dear God, grant me the wisdom to know... and do.

That person is like a tree planted by streams of water, which yields its fruit in season.
Psalm 1:3 NIV

261

Thank You, dear God, for all the creatures You have created to fill the earth. Around me I see birds and butterflies... frogs and fish... kittens and puppies. Let me, God, do everything in my power to make my corner of the world a safe and gentle, protected and loving place for **ANIMALS**.

God created...every living creature that moveth.
Genesis 1:21

262

So often I meet someone who is sad... who is mourning...who is down in the dumps. What can I do to **PULL UP** my friend? Empower me, dear God, with the courage to offer more than words, but to reach out in a real and practical way to help ease the sorrow of those encumbered with sadness.

I will not leave you comfortless: I will come to you.
John 14:18

263

Learning **LIFE'S LESSONS** isn't only for the young, but for everyone... including me. Dear God, grant me the humility I need to remain open to everything You have to teach me, and willingness to accept correction from others when I'm wrong. As long as there's life, there will be lessons to learn!

He that refuseth instruction despiseth his own soul.
Proverbs 15:32

264 Dear God, You intend people to travel life's **JOURNEY** together, hand-in-hand. Some of us hold the hand of a spouse, while others walk with loved ones, family, and friends. Grant, God, that everyone will come to know true companionship in this life.

A friend loveth at all times.
Proverbs 17:17

265 How high are my **ASPIRATIONS?** Do they reach beyond my easy grasp? Do they challenge me to stretch further... to look deeper... to discover more? Dear God, keep me from settling for second best, because You have made me first in Your heart and in Your love.

For every one that asketh receiveth; and he that seeketh findeth; and to him that knocketh it shall be opened.
Luke 11:10

266 In the darkness of my doubt and in the dim shadows of my understanding, I yearn for Your help, dear God. Lead me to someone who can minister to my spiritual needs... who is mature and experienced in Your ways. It is Your light I seek, God, for You are the **LIGHT OF THE WORLD.**

I am come a light into the world.
John 12:46

267 Being **REALISTIC** isn't always as easy as it sounds. Some people, terrified by obstacles, say it's unrealistic to even try to overcome them. Yes, dear God, I acknowledge the challenges ahead... but I also acknowledge the power You give to those who ask for it. That's the kind of realism I desire in my thinking and in my life.

Every mountain and hill shall be made low.
    Isaiah 40:4

268 Dear God, many people suffer need, and from the bottom of my heart I sympathize with their plight. Yet feelings of **SYMPATHY** do little to ease their hardships. Grant me the willingness and the wisdom to help others with the resources I have... to remember them in fervent prayer as well as in practical action.

Pray one for another.
    James 5:16

269 Why do I **STUBBORNLY CLING** to ways that don't work... to opinions proven to be false? God, grant me the inner strength and insight it takes to let go of lifelong habits that no longer fit my circumstances. Make me willing to change my thinking when evidence leads to a new conclusion. Let me let go, dear God, when I need to let go!

Be strong and of a good courage.
    Deuteronomy 31:6

270

Tomorrow. Yes, I tell myself "tomorrow" I'll eat healthy... spend less money... exercise more... visit a loved one. Yet I know from experience that "tomorrow" never comes. If it needs to be done, dear God, grant me the courage and determination to **START NOW**.

To day if ye will hear his voice,
harden not your hearts.
Hebrews 3:15

271

The power to **BLESS OTHERS** rests with all of us, dear God. Everyone—including me! You have given me the power of blessing, God, so let me use it today. I will bless those I meet with unconditional kindness and thoughtful words. I will bless them by assuring them of my prayers. I will bless them by remembering them with love.

The Lord be with you all.
2 Thessalonians 3:16

272

My friends are important to me, God, and now I realize the equal importance of being a **FRIEND TO MYSELF**. Keep me from telling myself things I would never say to others. Let my self-talk be as thoughtful, as supportive, as complimentary, and as gentle as the words I would share with a treasured friend. That, dear God, is the friend I want to be to myself.

Search me, O God, and know my heart.
Psalm 139:23

273

BROADEN MY UNDERSTANDING,
dear God, so I may know more about the world. Make
me wise in its ways so I can avoid becoming the victim
of those who would harm me or my loved ones. God,
bless me with the kind of understanding that sees with
discernment, with gentleness and in truth.

If any of you lack wisdom, let him ask of God.
James 1:5

274

Thank You, God, for the presence of **POSITIVE
PEOPLE** in my life. Bless those I name in my
heart today... those who bring happiness with them
wherever they go... those who lighten my heart
every time I see them. Just thinking about them
right now brings a smile to my face!

Rejoice evermore.
1 Thessalonians 5:16

275

What lies at the heart of happiness? Certainly
not money or things! While possessions make
our lives comfortable, they don't offer more than
temporary gladness. But lasting happiness is
available from You, God, and it doesn't cost a
penny. Rich or poor, I receive happiness by
embracing **SPIRITUAL THINGS**... things
I receive from You.

Having nothing, and yet possessing all things.
2 Corinthians 6:10

276 When I'm **TIRED**, dear God, make it possible for me to get the rest and relaxation I need. Despite my busy schedule and pressing responsibilities, help me find a way to set aside some quiet time. Through loving presence, refresh my heart and soul with the assurance of Your strength and power.

I will give you rest.
Matthew 11:28

277 You have given us the gift of humor to smooth the rough edges of life and lift the weight of daily challenges from us. Lighten my heart, dear God, so I may taste the sweetness of a smile on my lips and fill my hungry soul with the bread of levity and laughter. Grant me, God, the blessing of a **CHEERFUL HEART**.

Be glad in the LORD.
Psalm 32:11

278 Being a **LOVING PERSON** can be hard sometimes. Sure, I can act lovingly in certain circumstances, but to actually be a loving person with constancy and faithfulness takes more power than I possess. I pray, dear God, to grant me the strength and commitment I need to be a loving person in truth.

Love one another with a pure heart.
1 Peter 1:22

279

Dear God, I'm trying hard to **HANG ON**. Times are challenging, but I know the only way to win is to keep on going, keep on moving forward to the best of my ability. And with You by my side, God, I know it's not just me... it's the two of us together!

God is my strength and power.
2 Samuel 22:33

280

Giving money is easy compared to the challenge of **GIVING ONESELF**. To give myself, I need to clear my mind of my own thoughts. I need to turn off my cell phone and give my full attention to the voice of the person sitting across the table from me. Today, God, let me give of myself to another, as You have given Yourself to me.

It is more blessed to give than to receive.
Acts 20:35

281

How long has it been since I have actually marveled at something? Perhaps I am so used to seeing special effects on the movie screen that I find no thrill in the splendor of a sunrise, the vastness of the sea, the power of a storm, the soft spray of a summer rain? Dear God, show me again how to **MARVEL** at the "special effects" at work throughout nature.

This is the LORD's doing;
it is marvellous in our eyes.
Psalm 118:23

282 Economic news captures my attention. After all, I need a certain amount of money to meet my responsibilities and obligations... and You know that, dear God. You have promised to give me my "daily bread," and You do so through the gift of work and the blessing of providers in my life. Now I am free, God, to focus on the **TRUE RICHES** You give to me in abundance.

Set your affection on things above, not on things on the earth.
Colossians 3:2

283 When I meet infirm or elderly people who are still keenly **INTERESTED IN THE WORLD**, I'm heartened and inspired. They have discovered the fountain of youth, haven't they! Dear God, no matter how old I am or what my circumstances may be, grant me the willingness and commitment to remain passionate about life.

They go from strength to strength.
Psalm 84:7

284 Sometimes we wait too long to show how much we **CHERISH OTHERS**. Times change, and another opportunity never comes to say "I love you" or "Thank you for your presence in my life." Today, dear God, I promise to let at least one of my loved ones know how much they have always meant.

Time is short.
1 Corinthians 7:29

285 It would be difficult to live life without the gift of **RESILIENCE**. That's why I'm praying to You today for the ability to change when it's necessary, even if it means doing something much different than what I had expected. With the blessing of resilience, God, I'll be able to embrace every opportunity with joy.

Stand fast in the Lord.
Philippians 4:1

286 If I can't be one of life's movers and shakers, at least I can be **USEFUL**. I can volunteer for one of the jobs no one else seems to want. I can do something that doesn't get much attention, but needs doing nonetheless. Dear God, I'm determined to participate... to use my abilities... to work toward the common good.

Glory, honour, and peace, to every man that worketh good.
Romans 2:10

287 A **COMPLIMENT** always makes me feel good! I pray, dear God, that I remember to compliment others... to offer genuine praise for what I admire about them... to highlight their triumphs and successes. Let me share with others some of the wonderful feelings they so generously share with me when they pay me a compliment.

A word spoken in due season, how good is it!
Proverbs 15:23

288

Help me, dear God, **BREAK AWAY** from habits and addictions that are keeping me from living a healthy and joyful life. Too much time is spent on things I feel powerless to resist, and too much of my attention is trapped by faithless idols. God, I pray for strength to overcome these temptations.

The Lord stood with me.
2 Timothy 4:17

289

If I think there's nothing for me to do, all I need is a clear-eyed **LOOK AROUND**. There are those who need a caring person to respond to their calling out... there are projects in want of someone to move them forward with energy and commitment. Dear God, let me look around right now... and see.

Feed my sheep.
John 21:16

290

Among Your many promises, God, is the promise of forgiveness. No matter what burdens my heart... no matter what keeps me from lifting my eyes to heaven... I know I'll receive Your compassion and mercy the moment **I TURN TO YOU**. Today, God, my sole desire is to turn to You in truth.

Come, and let us return unto the LORD.
Hosea 6:1

291 When I'm faced with difficult choices, dear God, it's hard to **DO WHAT'S RIGHT**. I'm tempted to choose the easiest path... the road most comfortable and convenient for me. But it may not be the right thing to do, and I know it. Let me do what's right, God, knowing You are with me every step of the way.

Do good.
1 Peter 3:11

292 Sometimes I'm obliged to help, but my heart isn't in it. I feel I must, or I'm ashamed not to pitch in when others are watching. Though my attitude may not be apparent to all, I know it's apparent to You, because You look inside the heart. When I'm asked, dear God, grant me the blessing of being genuinely **GLAD TO HELP**.

Therefore, rid yourselves of all malice and all deceit, hypocrisy, envy, and slander of every kind.
1 Peter 2:1 NIV

293 They are only two words, but they make a world of difference: **THANK YOU**. Thank You, God, for the blessings You have sent me this day. And God, I will speak those two words again by saying "thank you" to others, especially to those around me... and to the people who share the day with me.

We give thanks to God and the Father of our Lord Jesus Christ.
Colossians 1:3

294 Most of us are aware of the damage our actions can cause the **ENVIRONMENT**...Your creation... the work of Your hands. But what can I do? Though I have neither the power nor the resources to rescue the world, I can make sure my corner of it is loved and cared for. This I can do, dear God, with Your help.

God himself that formed the earth and made it.
Isaiah 45:18

295 Anymore, it's so easy to **KEEP IN TOUCH!** We have gadgets that allow us to remain more connected than ever. Yet I want to do more than just update a website or drop an e-mail now and then. Dear God, let me spend the time it takes to really listen... to ask thoughtful questions... to truly share my stories and keep in touch with those I care about.

Love must be sincere.
Romans 12:9 NIV

296 I'm good about noting major milestones in the lives of others, God, but there are so many more times to **CELEBRATE**. There are the small triumphs that are so easily overlooked and ignored... yet it's such a special joy when someone else remembers. Let me, God, be the one who remembers.

Rejoice in the Lord always: and again I say, Rejoice.
Philippians 4:4

297 Dear God, I don't know all the answers... but I know You do. When I don't know the solution to a problem that affects me or challenges my thinking, grant me the willingness to **FIND OUT** more. You have blessed me with the resources I need to broaden my knowledge and deepen my understanding.

Call unto me, and I will answer thee, and show thee great and mighty things.
Jeremiah 33:3

298 I want to do more than just get by, dear God— I want to **DO MY BEST**. Though others may out-perform me, or even receive credit that belongs to me, I want to live knowing I have given my tasks my best work... my responsibilities my best effort. No, nothing I do will be perfect... but everything I do will get the best I have to give.

Whatsoever ye do, do it heartily, as to the Lord.
Colossians 3:23

299

MIRACLES happen every day, but God, I don't always see them. Open my eyes to better see You through the miracles at work all around me. Let me find You in the amazing healings, the special blessings, the "coincidences" so easily overlooked. Dear God, even if others put out alternative explanations, let me believe in Your miracles.

Remember his marvellous works that he hath done.
Psalm 105:5

300

True SATISFACTION in my life comes with accepting that You, God, are in control of it. Even when things are not going as I would prefer, I'm still satisfied, knowing You have a good purpose and plan in mind. No matter what my lack, I'm satisfied, because I have found my all in You.

Thou openest thine hand, and satisfiest
the desire of every living thing.
Psalm 145:16

301

Along with a good reputation, I want to possess **CREDIBILITY**. I want to shun hearsay and extremism, and embrace reason and moderation. Turn my attention to facts, dear God, so my comments are worthy of others' attention. Let my credibility stem from a heart and mind firmly based on the truth.

Sound speech, that cannot be condemned.
Titus 2:8

302 The words of scripture hold many mysteries for people, and God, I too have **QUESTIONS** about many things. Enable me to delve into scripture with a mind receptive to Your words, and allow Your message to take root in my heart. Grant me knowledge and understanding of Your words and ways.

How sweet are thy words unto my taste!
Psalm 119:103

303 My heart is burdened, dear God, with fears and misgivings about **THE FUTURE**. What will tomorrow bring? What is in store for me? Surround me, God, with Your comfort, and remove the weight of anxiety from me. Reassure me of Your presence, regardless of what the days and years may bring. Deepen my confidence in You.

Jesus Christ the same yesterday,
and to day, and for ever.
Hebrews 13:8

304 You **REVEAL** Yourself, God, to those who look for You. When I search for Your work in the world, I find it in the beauty of creation and in the miracles of love, friendship, courage, and compassion among people. As I look for You, dear God, show Yourself to me, and I will give thanks to You for all Your wonderful ways!

He is a rewarder of them that diligently seek him.
Hebrews 11:6

305 Why do people want to **PREDICT** the future? Only You, God, know all things to come, including the times and dates of major world happenings and events. I thank you, God, for today... and ask for Your guidance in living in this time and this place according to Your will for me.

The things of God knoweth no man.
1 Corinthians 2:11

306 Dear God, You offer **REFRESHMENT** for body and spirit. When I sit quietly listening for the whisper of Your voice in my heart, tension slips away... my body relaxes... my energy restored. My spirit is renewed, comforted by Your presence... enlivened by Your strength... embraced by Your love.

They that wait upon the LORD
shall renew their strength.
Isaiah 40:31

307 God, Your **REASONING** is not like my reasoning, limited to things of this world. Prevent me, dear Father, from using my human intellect to judge spiritual truths. Instead, let me be honest about what I don't understand, and trust in Your superior wisdom.

As the heavens are higher than the earth,
so are my ways higher than your ways,
and my thoughts than your thoughts.
Isaiah 55:9

308 You are gracious and merciful, dear God, and so I come to You today asking for Your guidance. When difficult choices come my way, help me hear Your answers and understand what You want for me. Then let me **REST AT EASE** with the direction I go, placing the outcome in Your hands.

Blessed is the man that trusteth in the LORD.
Jeremiah 17:7

309 **COMPROMISE** is necessary for smooth and cordial associations. Compromise is required for the effective working of organizations and governments. But, God, let me never compromise my faith. Keep me firm and unbending in matters concerning my relationship with You.

Stand firm. Let nothing move you.
1 Corinthians 15:58 NIV

310 It's uncomfortable for anyone to own up to wrongdoing...to admit personal weakness. Yet that's what You would have me do. Dear God, help me take responsibility for my words and actions. Whenever possible, I will make amends to anyone I have hurt. Grant me, dear God, the courage to hold myself **ACCOUNTABLE**.

I will confess my transgressions unto the LORD.
Psalm 32:5

311

As I think back to all the ways You have guided me and protected me over the years, dear God, I'm overwhelmed with thanks. Keep me in **REMEMBRANCE** of those times, knowing that what You have done for me in the past, You will continue to do now and in the future.

I will meditate also of all thy work,
and talk of thy doings.
Psalm 77:12

312

What do I really want? Just asking the question fills my mind with things I'd like to buy and blessings I'd like to possess. But far and above these desires, dear God, let my ultimate yearning become a desire for **GOOD**... the ability to see it, uphold it, and do it.

Do not forget to do good.
Hebrews 13:16 NIV

313

Wise leaders are few, but maybe even fewer are wise **FOLLOWERS**. A wise follower embraces humility, trust, and the ability to work side by side with others toward the common good. Most of all, a wise follower chooses carefully whom to follow. Dear God, help me be Your faithful follower.

If any man serve me, let him follow me.
John 12:26

314

Dear God, You are the source of goodness, kindness, joy, and love, and these are the **QUALITIES** I desire. In my words and actions, I want to express these qualities, and in my thoughts, I want to nurture them. Fill my heart, God, with all the gifts I need to grow in spiritual strength.

The fruit of the Spirit is love, joy, peace, longsuffering, gentleness, goodness, faith.
Galatians 5:22

315

Dear God, help me put the past behind me. I have learned valuable lessons from my experiences, and now it's time to move forward. Relieve my mind of **REGRET**–the "should haves" and "could haves" that serve only to hold me back. Enable me, God, to face today and every day ahead as a smarter, stronger, and wiser person.

Godly sorrow... leaves no regret.
2 Corinthians 7:10 NIV

316

Many people are careful with their money because they need to be; but I want to be **FRUGAL** because I want to be. I want to thank You, God, for my financial resources by not spending frivolously, but wisely and within my means. I want to be the one who can share with an open hand and willing heart because I practice frugality.

God loveth a cheerful giver.
2 Corinthians 9:7

317

In most all walks of life, we meet people from different backgrounds, with various abilities, talents, and outlooks. Grant me the ability to genuinely welcome **DIVERSITY**... to learn from those who can teach me, and to serve as a good example for those who would learn from me. Never let our differences, God, hide the beauty of our common humanity.

And all ye are brethren.
Matthew 23:8

318

Dear God, how happy I am because You are **ALIVE IN ME!** How can I weep when my heart is open to the delights of Your creation? How can I despair when I know that my loving and compassionate God is right beside me? Let my heart express its joy... let me relax in You and be happy today!

All that hear will laugh with me.
Genesis 21:6

319

When I'm confused, I want to get down to **ESSENTIALS**. That's what I do when I'm not sure what to believe, or I'm baffled by conflicting claims. Essentials are those things You have set as the foundation for faith: a decision to welcome You into my heart and my life, and a grateful acceptance of Your presence.

Be not afraid, only believe.
Mark 5:36

320 Not everyone is **LOYAL**, but You are, dear God. Your loyalty spans the generations, from the beginning of time until now. Your loyalty stands, even when people dismiss You and turn away from You. It's Your loyalty, God, that quiets my fears and takes away my worries. In all things, let me be loyal to others in their need.

Faithful is he that calleth you.
1 Thessalonians 5:24

321 In my life, dear God, help me formulate **CORE VALUES** that I will not violate under any circumstances. These values... fairness, compassion, forgiveness, love, to name a few... give me stable ground to stand on when I'm confronted by moral and ethical dilemmas. Positive core values direct my actions and thinking according to Your will.

The integrity of the upright shall guide them.
Proverbs 11:3

322 Some people say they want to believe in You, God, but not until after they discover You. I have found a better way: change my **BEHAVIOR** first, and I begin to discover You. As my actions become more kind and loving, Your work in my heart deepens my faith and understanding. This is how, dear God, I am coming to find out who You are.

We walk by faith, not by sight.
2 Corinthians 5:7

323 Thank You, God, for **GOOD PEOPLE!**
They're the ones who willingly and generously
help out wherever there's a need... whether it's doing
a small favor for a neighbor, or pitching in to aid
a whole community affected by disaster. Grant me the
readiness, dear God, to count myself among them!

The earth is full of the goodness of the LORD.
Psalm 33:5

324 God, grant me the gift of **ATTRACTIVENESS**
to others. I don't mean possessing movie-star good
looks or celebrity charisma... but practicing the al-
lure of a pleasant smile, a gentle attitude,
and a caring heart. This kind of attractiveness
is appealing to people... and to You.

The LORD looketh on the heart.
1 Samuel 16:7

325 God, You have made Your feelings toward me clear:
You love me unconditionally. That knowledge gives
me the **FREEDOM** to live a joyous life. I do not
need to worry about saving up "good behavior"
points to earn Your love, because You are already
pleased with me and Your love for me is great! I
have the freedom to follow You, not because of fear,
but because of love.

And I will walk at liberty.
Psalm 119:45

326

Sometimes I find myself expecting the worst. I imagine sickness, setbacks, and disappointment waiting for me just around the corner! From today forward, dear God, help me replace pictures of peril with projections of delight... with the joy of happy outcomes... with strength to bear in times of trouble. Let me live in the **EXPECTATION** of Your gracious hand at work in all things.

For I know the thoughts that I think toward you, saith the LORD, thoughts of peace.
Jeremiah 29:11

327

No matter where I am in life, dear God, grant me the willingness to focus on **IMPROVEMENT**. Show me what practical steps I can take today to improve my interactions with others... upgrade my skills and expand my knowledge... grow and mature in handling daily matters in a way that is pleasing to You. Let me see improvement and earn its reward.

Let not your hands be weak: for your work shall be rewarded.
2 Chronicles 15:7

328

The gift of **EMPATHY** allows me to put myself in the shoes of others... to open my heart to them so I not only understand, but feel, their humanity. Grant me, dear God, the willingness to become one with others wherever they are... and to show compassion to them, whoever they may be.

Remember them that are in bonds,
as bound with them.
Hebrews 13:3

329

Part of knowing who I am is remembering my roots. Thank You, dear God, for the **HERITAGE** that is mine. Neither let me be ashamed of those who have gone before me, nor let me boast of their achievements as my own. Rather, God, let my life bless my family today and contribute to a good heritage for all.

I have a goodly heritage.
Psalm 16:6

330

I'm inspired by those who have little, yet share generously...who face immense difficulties, yet shun self-pity...who are looked down on by others, yet retain their **DIGNITY**. Grant me, dear God, the faith and endurance I need to face difficult circumstances with dignity and poise.

The God of heaven, he will prosper us.
Nehemiah 2:20

331 Dear God, grant me the generosity of spirit I need to give **CREDIT** where credit is due. In a spirit of genuine fellowship, let my congratulations encourage and support those whose achievements may surpass mine... whose efforts inspire all to focus on excellence.

Whoever refreshes others will be refreshed.
Proverbs 11:25 NIV

332 It's **ATTITUDE**, not age, that makes a person old. Dear God, help me celebrate every birthday not with dread, but with gratitude for another year of growing closer to You. Grant me the blessing of a youthful heart and a vibrant spirit... then no matter how many candles appear on my cake, I will always enjoy the newness of life.

To be spiritually minded is life and peace.
Romans 8:6

333 It would be impossible to play on a team if there were no **RULES** to the game. What chaos on the field! In the same way, living without Your commandments would have me running in all directions and not knowing if I'm doing the right thing. This is just a little prayer of thanks, God, for setting up the rules of life.

Blessed is the man that feareth the LORD,
that delighteth greatly in his commandments.
Psalm 112:1

334 Dear God, even should I choose to **ABANDON** You, You will never abandon me. Though there are times I think You are gone from my life, it is only my spiritual darkness, not the absence of Your light. Let me stand on the promise of Your presence, God, until the shadows are gone and a new dawn has come.

Nor height, nor depth, nor any other creature,
shall be able to separate us from the love of God.
Romans 8:39

335 When my circumstances are not serving me well, grant me, dear God, the readiness to look for **OTHER POSSIBILITIES**. Give me the motivation and initiative I need to ask probing questions, find out about viable options, and take appropriate action. There are other possibilities, and with You as my guide, I can take advantage of them.

Thou shalt guide me with thy counsel.
Psalm 73:24

336 When I speak of You to others, dear God, I need only tell them what I know about You. I'm not required to answer every tough question or engage in theological discussions I can't handle. Grant me the willingness and the courage to share my faith by speaking of my actual **EXPERIENCE** with You.

One thing I know, that, whereas I was blind, now I see.
John 9:25

337 After a number of successes, it's tempting to sit back and enjoy my position. Yet to remain successful, I need to be **PREPARED** for the next project... the next challenge... the next place I can make a difference. In my spiritual life, dear God, let me stay ready and prepared for the next step along the way.

I can do all things through Christ which strengtheneth me.
Philippians 4:13

338

Dear God, at certain times of my life, I have felt **CLOSE TO YOU**. Your presence engaged my senses, and I had no doubt You were with me at that moment. Help me use what I know about those times to bring the reality of Your presence home to me now. Grant me, God, the blessing of You.

It is good for me to draw near to God.
Psalm 73:28

339

I value the wisdom I have received from those who have gone before me. Their words are my most prized inheritance. To all of us, God, You leave the wisdom of scripture...Your **LEGACY** of love to those who follow You and listen to Your voice. Thank You, God, for Your great gift!

Let the word of Christ dwell in you richly in all wisdom.
Colossians 3:16

340

I read about someone who's making a real difference in the world, and I'm **INSPIRED**. Yet there are things I can do that won't make headlines, but will lift up... encourage... strengthen... help. Enable me, dear God, to do these things... not because I'll make the news today, but because I'll make a difference in someone's life.

Let another man praise thee, and not thine own mouth.
Proverbs 27:2

341

It has been said, "Feed your faith and your doubts will starve to death." How true! The more I meditate on Your truths, God, the more I'm **CONVINCED** of Your loving kindness, Your compassion, and Your great love for me. To keep healthy spiritually, I need You every day.

Meditate upon these things.
1 Timothy 4:15

342

I take so many things for granted. I wake up in the morning, shower, eat breakfast, and go about the activities of my day. Yet I realize many people are unable to do these things, and so much of what I have are **LUXURIES** others can only dream about. Starting with the privilege of life and breath, dear God, I thank You for everything I have today.

Blessed be the Lord, who daily loadeth us with benefits.
Psalm 68:19

343

Sometimes I get impatient with people. I get tired of forgiving them so often, and I yearn to yell, "This is the last time!" But then I remember something, God: this isn't the way You treat me. You offer me forgiveness **EVERY TIME** I come to You with a sincere heart... even if it's for the same old mistake. Let this be my attitude with others.

Bear with each other and forgive one another.
Colossians 3:13 NIV

344

To work effectively, I need to get **ORGANIZED**. Dear God, help me learn to take control of my time, make realistic plans, and tend to my most important tasks first. Let me begin today by organizing my time so You are first... and preparing whatever I need to fulfill my responsibilities.

Everything should be done in a fitting and orderly way.
1 Corinthians 14:40 NIV

345

No matter how little I think I have, I possess more than many other people. Dear God, with a heart filled with gratitude for my blessings, let me **GIVE BACK** where I can. Help me take advantage of opportunities to show others how much I care and to return thanks for everything You have given me.

Those who are kind benefit themselves.
Proverbs 11:17 NIV

346

When things aren't going my way, I start **FEELING DEFEATED**. I wonder if I'm able to manage everything in front of me, and I'm afraid I won't be able to hold out much longer. Dear God, what should I do? Lead me to experience Your strength. Open to me hope for a better day to come.

He heard me, and delivered me from all my fears.
Psalm 34:4

347

When someone does a favor for me, I say "thank you"... but then forget the incident. It takes a back seat to my problems and complaints. Help me, dear God, to value the **THOUGHTFULNESS OF OTHERS** that their actions become the high point in my day. With their kindness in mind, let me pass it on!

The merciful man doeth good to his own soul.
Proverbs 11:17

348

Not everyone enjoys physical **VITALITY**, but spiritual vitality is open to all. Though my body is prone to sickness and ill-health, renew and refresh my spirit, dear God. Keep my spirit strong and eager, flexible and teachable. No matter what outer conditions afflict me, let my inner health remain vibrant.

If any man thirst, let him come unto me, and drink.
John 7:37

349 I think I can tell a **MODEST** garment from an immodest one; but more important than the cut of clothes is having a modest attitude. Dear God, this is the kind of attitude You approve of, for it is humble, gracious, and peaceful. It is never boastful or proud. Enable me, God, to clothe my heart with a spirit such as this.

For everyone who exalts himself will be humbled, and he who humbles himself will be exalted.
Luke 14:11 NIV

350 I shake my head in disbelief when I hear of someone attempting a dangerous stunt. Yet, living life without You, God, is the most dangerous "stunt" anyone could dare to try. Keep me from the **ARROGANCE** of thinking I could pull it off, because I couldn't. Keep me, I pray, in the security of Your arms.

Whoso putteth his trust in the LORD shall be safe.
Proverbs 29:25

351 Let my **SPIRIT SOAR**, dear God! Let me discover the magnificence of the world You have created and the uniqueness of myself and those around me. Loose my aspirations and ignite my dreams... because You have given me the wings of imagination, God, so I can fly to the heights.

God hath set the land before thee:
go up and possess it.
> Deuteronomy 1:21

352 Dear God, teach me how to **SPEAK UP** for myself when the need arises. Don't let a show of self-importance or the scorn of a bully intimidate me. Rather, open my mouth to say those words that insist on respect and dignity for myself... the same respect and dignity I readily give to others.

Lift up thy voice with strength;
lift it up, be not afraid.
> Isaiah 40:9

353 Sometimes I just want to **PRAISE** You, God! I want to sit in Your presence and simply tell You how glad I am that You put me on this Earth and opened to me the marvelous adventure of life. Most of all, I want to thank You for being my God and for the relationship I have with You.

All that is within me, bless his holy name.
Psalm 103:1

354 Dear God, without You, I feel like a ship adrift on a stormy sea. The winds of my feelings and emotions blow me this way and that way, and I'm not getting anywhere. Come into my life, God, and **STEER ME** through these rough waters. Bring me to the calm harbor of Your love.

He arose, and rebuked the winds and the sea; and there was a great calm.
Matthew 8:26

355 Life comes with no **GUARANTEES**, but it does come with Your promises, God. While I'm not guaranteed an easy life, I am promised Your help all the way through it. Though I'm not guaranteed everything I want, I am promised everything I need to remain spiritually alive and healthy. Your promises, God, are all I require.

The Lord is not slack concerning his promise.
2 Peter 3:9

356 Some people like a good **MYSTERY**. Yet even the most avid mystery fan could never arrive at a full knowledge of You and Your work! This side of heaven, I'll be content with the clues You leave... the wonder of the human body, the magnificence of nature, the peace of mind that comes with Your constant presence.

The peace of God, which passeth all understanding, shall keep your hearts and minds through Christ Jesus.
Philippians 4:7

357 The **GOLDEN RULE** may be well-known, but it isn't always well-followed, is it, God? Grant me the willingness, dear God, to do to others as I would like them to do to me. That includes how I talk about them... how I assess their personal qualities... how eager I am to help them when they need it. Enable me to follow the Golden Rule in my life.

As ye would that men should do to you, do ye also to them likewise.
Luke 6:31

358 There are times when I need to **SAY NO**, but I lack the courage. Instead, I make myself as inconspicuous as possible until I can find a way out. Next time, dear God, let my "no" resound loudly and clearly. Enable me to stand up for myself and what I know is the right thing to do.

The joy of the LORD is your strength.
Nehemiah 8:10

359 There are times when I need to **SAY YES**, but I hesitate to commit myself. Instead, I hedge and hope the question will be forgotten. Next time, dear God, let my "yes" resound loudly and clearly. Enable me to step forward in confidence and to carry out my commitment with faithfulness, care, and attention.

Choose the good.
Isaiah 7:15

360 Because I believe in You, it doesn't mean I'll never **WEEP**... it just means I'll weep without despair. I'll weep because I feel sad, but I'll weep knowing my sadness is temporary. You, dear God, give me strength to bear disappointment and loss; You, dear God, are the source of my comfort and hope.

The LORD hath heard the voice of my weeping.
Psalm 6:8

361

Somehow I seem to get pulled into **ARGUMENTS**. I'm hurt by the angry words I hear, and the ones I say hurt others. Enable me, dear God, to stop arguments before they get going. Grant me the wisdom to step out of the role I've been playing and find other ways to solve problems. Having an argumentative nature doesn't help... it hurts.

Follow peace with all men.
Hebrews 12:14

362

Dear God, empower me to avoid those things that threaten my spiritual health and well-being. Keep me from pitfalls, such as ill-advised choices and impulsive behavior. Instead, let my thoughts, words, and conduct together keep me on the **GOOD PATH** You have laid out for me.

Thou wilt shew me the path of life.
Psalm 16:11

363 I have a desire, dear God, to get back at the person who has wronged me. Yet I know that **REVENGE** is not mine to give. Turn my heart away from thoughts of revenge and toward what You would have me to do. From the bottom of my heart, God, let me bless the person whose name comes to mind as I pray...

Do not seek revenge or bear a grudge against anyone.
Leviticus 19:18 NIV

364 When things don't go my way, I tend to see only what's wrong with what happened. Grant me the ability, to accept the **REAL OUTCOME**, dear God. Even more, let me find the good in it, use the opportunities it offers, and continue to grow in knowledge and experience.

Trust in the LORD with all thine heart.
Proverbs 3:5

365 Prayers are like F**OOTSTEPS** leading me closer to You, dear God. May each prayer of mine deepen my trust in You and understanding of Your ways. May my prayers for others ask Your blessing upon them, and inspire me to bring Your love to them in word and action. For this I pray, dear God!

You provide a broad path for my feet.
2 Samuel 22:37 NIV